RAISING GENERATION TECH

PREPARING YOUR

CHILDREN FOR A

MEDIA-FUELED WORLD

JIM TAYLOR, PhD

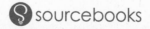
sourcebooks

Published by Sourcebooks, Inc.
P.O. Box 4410, Naperville, Illinois 60567-4410
(630) 961-3900
Fax: (630) 961-2168
www.sourcebooks.com

Library of Congress Cataloging-in-Publication Data

Taylor, Jim
  Raising generation tech : preparing your children for a media-fueled world / Jim Taylor.
       p. cm.
  Includes bibliographical references and index.
  1. Internet and youth. 2. Technology and youth. 3. Parenting. I. Title.
  HQ799.9.I58T39 2012
  004.67'80835—dc23

                              2012016920

Printed and bound in the United States of America.
VP 10 9 8 7 6 5 4 3 2 1

Raising Generation Tech is my twelfth book. I, of course, have dedicated my books to all the people who have supported me through the publication of each one over the years. To be honest, in this twelfth publication, I'm finding it difficult to create individual heartfelt and pithy dedications to everyone again.

So, hopefully without detracting from the individual contributions that each one has made to my writing of *Raising Generation Tech*, I dedicate it to all of them en masse: to my publisher, Sourcebooks; my editor, Peter Lynch; my agent, Carol Mann; my friend and mentor Gerry Sindell; my father and late mother, Shel and Ceci Taylor; and my sister, Heidi. Without your experience, knowledge, insight, patience, support, and love, my vision of *Raising Generation Tech* would not have become a reality. Plus, a special dedication to my wife, Sarah, and my daughters, Catie and Gracie. Without you, my life would not be complete.

CONTENTS

Introduction   1

Part I: This Crazy New World   23

Chapter 1: Popular Culture Today   25

Chapter 2: Technology Today   33

Chapter 3: Setting Defaults in Your Children   53

Chapter 4: An Unmediated Life Worth Living   63

Part II: Protect and Prepare Your Children   73

Chapter 5: Self-Identity: Who Are They?   75

Chapter 6: Values: What Do Your Children Believe?   93

Chapter 7: Thinking: What's on Their Minds?   117

Chapter 8: Relationships: How Connected Are They?   145

Chapter 9: Health: Use It or Lose It?   167

Chapter 10: Life: What's It All Mean?   189

Part III: The Hard Work and the Payoff   207

Chapter 11: Do the Job You Signed Up For   209

Chapter 12: Meet Your Kids 3.0   231

Afterword   255

References   257

Acknowledgments   277

Index   279

About the Author   293

Introduction

Our children are growing up in a world that is vastly different from the one in which we were raised. Economically, politically, socially, culturally, and technologically, the world that we live in hardly resembles the world of just a few decades ago. Consider this: Facebook and text messaging, two of the most popular and powerful forces in the lives of young people today, didn't even exist ten years ago. The Internet itself has only been in widespread use for around fifteen years.

The vast changes that we have observed over the past few decades are certainly unsettling for us "digital immigrants." We may worry about what the world will look like in the coming years and long for a simpler and slower time (although the "good old days" were probably not as good as we remember them). At the same time, for our children—the "digital natives"—this crazy new world is neither crazy nor new; it's just their world, and it's filled with excitement and possibilities. Regardless of where you are standing, one thing is certain: there is no going back. Technology is an inexorable force that can't be stopped, nor should we want it to be.

People, however, haven't changed much. Despite the immense changes that have transpired throughout time, we humans are little different from our ancestors of thousands of years ago. That seemingly obvious fact may no longer be fact from here on in. New technology is altering us as individuals, changing our brain development and functioning, and as a society, reweaving the social and cultural webs (no pun intended) that encircle our lives.

The challenge for us as parents is to ensure that these dramatic changes help foster a better world for our children and that our children are well equipped to master the increasingly complex world that they will inhabit. This challenge is no small matter. As the visionary educator and philosopher Marshall McLuhan said almost half a century ago, "We shape our tools and afterwards our tools shape us." That sentiment predated computers, mobile phones, and the Internet. As if looking into a crystal ball, McLuhan saw the future. For us and especially for our children, that future is now.

The speed at which technological advancement is occurring is so breakneck that we have little time to consider the implications of each new development before the latest technology takes root in our collective psyches. Only looking in our rearview mirror can we begin to understand how these new technologies have altered the way we think, the way we connect, and ultimately who we are. Only then are we able to judge whether those changes are beneficial or detrimental, but by then, it's too late to undo the changes. The relentless pace of innovation forces us to play a constant game of catch-up that we have little chance of winning.

As someone who has serious concerns about the influence of technology on children (and on all of us), I'll admit that I may sound like Chicken Little. Calls of "The sky is falling" have been heard throughout the history of technological advancement, for example, with the introduction of writing during the Bronze Age and the invention of the printing press in the 1400s. Yet, in most of these cases, these game changers have been boons to humanity rather than the end of days that those Chicken Littles predicted. Plus, we as humans have shown ourselves to be remarkably adaptable creatures who can readily adjust to the variety of changes with which we've been confronted.

The essential question is whether this pattern of Chicken Little reactions to technological changes is an appropriate response or whether simple acceptance of the inevitable is perfectly reasonable. If the metaphor holds true to form, then I would argue that, given the poor track record of calls about the end of the world, Chicken Little should be kept in his coop. At the other end of the continuum, though, blithe submission also seems misguided, particularly given the growing body of research showing that technology can have a negative impact on our lives. As with most things in life, the best answer usually lies somewhere in the middle of the two extremes. As the saying goes, better safe than sorry.

With this book, we can draw some compelling conclusions from emerging research and from what we see occurring before our very eyes. My intention is not to act as Chicken Little but rather to sound an alarm. My goal is not to repel technology; it's to help you use technology and the culture it creates to your children's greatest advantage.

The Power of Popular Culture

There has always been popular culture. Various media, however primitive by today's standards, have always influenced the way we think, feel, and behave, and how we communicate and interact with others.

Popular culture has been defined as a reflection of the values, norms, and beliefs held by the people in a particular culture. When certain ideas, interests, or choices reach a critical mass within a society, they become widely accepted and proliferate throughout that society. Most people think of popular culture as the most common forms of entertainment, whether television, movies, music, or what's on the Web. Those are really just the conduits through which popular culture is expressed.

Popular culture actually plays a vital role in maintaining a vigorous society and a healthy democracy. Collectively, a popular culture that is an expression of a society's shared experiences has essential value and a beneficial function to that society. Perhaps as much as the rule of law, an authentic popular culture acts as a societal truth, a shared bond that holds societies together and communicates that "we are one." Maybe more powerfully than the top-down government-provided glue, a genuine popular culture, created "of the people, by the people, and for the people," acts as the real, bottom-up glue that unites diverse people into a cohesive society.

As individuals, a genuine popular culture instills a sense of ownership and empowerment in our society because each of us knows that we contribute to that culture. We are more likely to act in our society's best interests because we know that those best interests are also our own. An authentic popular culture also gives us a sense of shared identity, meaning, and purpose that transcends differences in geography, race, ethnicity, religion, or politics. All of these then encourage us to lead a life in accordance with our culture's values and norms because they are our own.

Popular culture was, until the electronic revolution, an organic expression of what the populace of a society found engaging and that had the unifying effect that I just described. Yes, forces outside of "the people" have always tried to sway the masses, whether through soapbox proselytizing or ads in early print media, but the influence of those forces was obviously tempered by their limited reach.

Then radio, television, and movies were invented, and the ability of inorganic forces to influence popular sentiment and, by extension, popular culture, grew exponentially. With this powerful new technology, this impact wasn't restricted to face-to-face contact or small geographical regions in which newspapers and other print media were distributed. Its impact reached across miles and states, and now, of course, it extends nationwide and internationally. That reach has also changed what *popular culture* means.

With this ability to reach increasingly larger audiences, businesses saw these electronic media as conduits through which they could sell their goods and services. They also saw how they could directly influence a society's values, norms, and beliefs in ways that would encourage sales and increase revenues. Advertising became more and more sophisticated in its ability to shape and, yes, manipulate the needs and wants of its audience. That impact has grown exponentially with the rise of the Internet to the point that, through the latest computer and communications technology, children (and all of us) can be exposed to these influences almost every hour of the waking day.

The result has been the loss of an authentic popular culture, one that is a reflection of what "the people" value, and the emergence of a synthetic culture that is driven by the forces of materialism and consumerism. As a commenter on one of my blogs observed, there is nothing popular about popular culture these days: "[Most] of what is considered popular culture is churned out by corporations…with the sole purpose…that we can be converted into voracious consumers." We didn't demand, for example, *American Idol, Grand Theft Auto*, or Facebook. They were created to make money and then marketed as "must-haves," which, admittedly, the masses then embraced, and then they became a part of our so-called popular culture.

This synthetic culture not only has significant implications for our society as a whole but also has serious ramifications for how children develop. An essential purpose of popular culture is to enculturate children into society by communicating to them accepted values, norms, attitudes, and beliefs. The intent of this process is to prepare children to be functioning and contributing members of that society.

Yet, when children grow up in a synthetic culture that is far removed from the realities of society, they are prevented from learning what it takes to survive and thrive in that society. In addition, this synthetic culture isn't nurturing, because it doesn't care at all about children. It is downright disorienting to children because of the large chasm that lies between that artificial culture and the genuine and caring culture that they need to feel safe and secure. This unsettling experience is exacerbated by children's inability to distinguish between what is authentic and what is manufactured.

This synthetic culture is also suffocating genuine popular culture, depriving it of the oxygen it needs to live and flourish. Today's parents, who were raised in a predominantly authentic popular culture in which media and technology was less evident and influential in their lives (there wasn't the ubiquity of TV channels, radio stations, magazines, shopping malls, and advertising—and, of course, there was no Internet), are the only link that this generation of children has to anything other than the current synthetic culture. What is perhaps more disturbing is the realization that, if this synthetic culture continues to dominate our societal landscape, the next generation of children may have no connection to authentic popular culture. What is now a clearly manufactured culture will simply become popular culture for future generations.

It is these forces that our generation of parents must confront while raising our children, forces that no other generation had to confront previously. The melding of this synthetic popular culture with technology has created a new world, one that feels so alien and different from the world in which we grew up. It is our responsibility as parents to help our children not only to survive but also to thrive in this crazy new world while preserving whatever authentic popular culture we have left.

The Power of Technology

A central belief that I want to convey in *Raising Generation Tech* is that technology may be the most powerful force in society today, and as the noted technology historian Melvin Kranzberg observes in his six laws of technology, "Technology is neither good nor bad—nor is it neutral." Technology isn't neutral, because it does, clearly, have an impact on our lives. The nature of that impact is what determines whether technology is good or bad.

When I speak about technology, I am casting a wide net that encompasses gadgetry both quite old and very new. Technology includes oh-so-twentieth-century media such as movies, radio, and television. It also includes more recent developments in computers (e.g., desktops, laptops, tablets) and communications (e.g., mobile phones, GPS). Technology, in its latest iteration, comprises the Internet, and the entire universe of information, connectivity, and devices at our children's fingertips.

Technology influences your children (and you) both indirectly and directly. First, it acts as a conduit through which our popular culture inserts itself into your children's lives. Popular culture has certainly changed over the past two decades, but the means by which it can reach children has changed even more. Thanks to the proliferation of communication technology, which has grown exponentially in the past twenty years—for example, the birth of the Internet, the proliferation of smartphones, the emergence of viral marketing, and the explosion of social media—popular culture is now an almost inescapable presence in your children's lives; it influences them more often, more directly, and more powerfully than ever before.

Second, as Marshall McLuhan suggested so presciently in 1964, "the medium is the message," which means that, beyond the content that is conveyed, the medium itself has an impact by its very nature and unique characteristics. For example, the use of social media means that we have less need to interact with others directly. This distancing of communication has real implications for children's development. If learning to communicate with others is a skill that develops with practice, children's constant use of social media reduces the experiences they have with which to learn social skills. McLuhan asserts that we are so focused on the content of the technology that we neglect to notice the influence of the technology itself on people. This observation is certainly true today: we focus on what the technology provides (e.g., video, text messages, social media), but we fail to consider how the very act of using these advances shapes us.

All the developments in technology of the past two decades affect our children in so many ways, including cognitively, socially, culturally, politically, and physically. Researchers in such diverse fields as computer science, psychology, sociology, philosophy, and the neurosciences are only beginning to explore these medium-not-content issues and to study how McLuhan's thesis applies to the most recent technological developments. Frighteningly, early investigations on the impact of technology on children have indicated that many parents whose children are, as digital natives, immersed in technology, don't even consider the ramifications of either the content or the medium on their children's development.

The Power of Parents

So what are we as parents to do so our children don't become zombies of this synthetic culture or drown in the tsunami of technology that is overwhelming them? We can't turn back the clock. We can't raise our children in caves. We can't teach them that popular culture or technology are evil, because neither is. Popular culture can be a wonderful source of entertainment. Technology is just a tool, and it is what we do with it that determines whether it helps or hurts our children.

At the same time, we can't just sit back and let our children be influenced willy-nilly by popular culture and technology. To do so would be to naively believe that both have only benefits and no costs. To do so would put our children at the mercy of the manipulations of popular culture and the uncertainty and capriciousness of technology. Such an attitude would place far too great an onus on our children to decide which elements of popular culture they want to be exposed to and which technology to use and how to use it. It would place an unrealistic amount of trust in our children that they have the capacity to distinguish the benefits from the costs of popular culture and technology.

To add insult to parental injury, because of the growing impact of popular culture and technology, we just don't have the influence over our children that we once had. In generations past, parents had an easier time controlling their children's lives (in a good sense) because there were fewer outside forces trying to insert themselves into their families' lives. Homes used to be largely impervious to the cultural "elements" (radio and television were the greatest intrusions); now, homes are largely permeable, with cable wiring and satellite transmissions breaching the literal and metaphorical membrane that exists between home and the world beyond its walls.

I also think it's important at this point to define what I mean by *children*, because the term can encompass a wide range, from newborns to the late teens (in fact, they'll always be our children, no matter how old they are). Certainly, it's never too early to begin guiding and directing your children's exposure to popular culture and their use of technology. For example, many parents these days give their children access to tablets and smartphones before they can walk or talk, whereas other parents actively limit this exposure.

At the same time, it's never too late to exert this influence over your children. Because children don't come with owner's manuals, we often just muddle through raising our children without knowing whether or not our approach works, until it seems like it's too late. But be assured that it's never too late. If you see that something you are doing or allowing your older children to do is unhealthy, it is your right, responsibility, and absolute moral imperative to make changes. Of course, your children may not like those changes at first, but, as I will discuss later, if you are committed to the changes, your children will probably come around.

A Complex Relationship

The relationship among technology, popular culture, and children's development is complex and difficult to define. Because both our boots-on-the-ground experience and research studying this issue are still relatively limited, there continues to be little clarity on the role that they play in children's development. As a result, we cannot easily label this influence "good" or "bad," "healthy" or "unhealthy." There are, however, four questions that can help determine the degree of influence that popular culture and technology have on children and whether that influence is constructive or detrimental:

1. How often are your children exposed to popular culture and immersed in technology?
2. What is the quality of content to which they are exposed?
3. To what degree do you provide limits and guidance in your children's interactions in popular culture and technology?
4. How much counterbalancing exposure do your children get from positive influences and experiences?

As we explore the role of popular culture and technology in your children's lives, you should use these four questions to help judge whether popular culture and technology are beneficial or harmful to their development.

Children as Software

I believe that children can be compared to the evolving versions of software, which is why I chose the term Kids 3.0 to describe children who are optimally prepared to thrive in this increasingly complex world. First, because *Raising Generation Tech* is not only about the meeting of children and technology, but also about what seems like their integration, the metaphor seemed appropriate. I saw significant parallels between the development of software and children's development. The latest versions of software are intended to be new and improved, with better functionality and fewer glitches and bugs. The same is true with the development of children. A key goal of *Raising Generation Tech* is to ensure that children's immersion in this new technology results in their being new and improved rather than "buggy," for example, children making bad decisions, or, even worse, having a "virus" that cripples them, such as children adopting bad values that lead them down an unhealthy road. Parents have perhaps the most essential role in whether children's entry into this connected world of popular culture and technology results in a version upgrade (i.e., a meaningful and fulfilling life) or a software that crashes (i.e., a life of struggles and dissatisfaction).

That's not to say that I extend this metaphor too far by viewing children as unfeeling, calculating little bundles of code. To the contrary, what makes children so receptive to the wonders that this new technology has to offer and susceptible to potential harm that it might cause is that they are vulnerable beings who are open to so many different kinds of inputs.

The evolution of the Web from version 1.0 to its yet-to-be-released version 3.0 also has striking parallels to the development of children. Web 1.0 tended to be static and one dimensional in its flow of information. It typically had a simple design and rudimentary functionality. Web 1.0 was also controlled by the relatively few who had the ability to create and provide content. Similarly, babies, that is to say, Kids 1.0, have limited ability to interact, and most of the information flows from the external world to them. Plus, they are relatively simple, with little or no "functionality," and parents have primary control over what their children experience.

Web 2.0 is characterized by greater user participation and freedom, idea creation, collaboration, and democratization of content. Importantly, the Web became a social force in which people can interact with one another directly. It also opened the door to less positive influences, such as spammers and pornographers, who use the openness of the Web for nefarious and destructive purposes. In a similar vein, the toddler and preschool years are highlighted by the increased ability to actively participate in life's activities, have a say in one's own life, and develop more complex relationships. As they are exposed more to the outside world, young children also become vulnerable to less constructive influences from those beyond their immediate families.

Finally, Web 3.0—which, by the way, doesn't yet exist but is expected to emerge within the coming decade—offers users total and continuous connectivity, with constant access to information, complete interactivity, immediate and widespread social networking, and a convergence between the real world and cyber worlds. By the same token, as children enter elementary school today, they experience a growing convergence between their internal world and the larger world of information, relationships, and popular culture. Their identities will become inextricably linked to and woven into the greater social fabric of this larger world.

Web 3.0 will also offer more bandwidth, which means that it will be able to offer more information more quickly to an almost limitless audience. As children develop, they too gain greater bandwidth, or the ability to process information of greater complexity with increased speed.

By the way, there is already talk of Web 4.0, which, I am quite sure, will have new, unforeseen, and even more challenging influences on how children develop. We as parents will have our hands full just dealing with the impending release of Web 3.0, so, as the saying goes, let's cross that bridge when we come to it.

Who Are Kids 3.0?

There are certain qualities that children must develop to take control of the connected world in which they are growing up. This book will help you help your children develop these qualities, which have always been essential to children's development but are perhaps even more important in this crazy new world. These very same qualities are threatened by the negative and unintended side effects of popular culture and new technology, and as a result, they are more difficult for parents today to develop in their children.

The sad irony is that many parents expose their children to technology early and often with the belief that it will better prepare them for success in the digital world. In reality, they are actually doing their children a disservice by causing their minds to become programmed in ways that actually limit them in both the digital and the corporeal worlds.

Think about the kinds of people you want your children to become. What values, attitudes, and skills will they need for this next "version" of life? Then look at the world they are growing up in, and ask yourself whether this world supports or interferes with the development of those people. Although there are many attributes that are important for children's healthy development, the six qualities that I focus on in *Raising Generation Tech*—values, self-identity, thinking, relationships, health, and life—seem to me to be most vulnerable to the "dark side" of popular culture and technology. Not only are these six areas not nurtured by the connected, 24/7 world, but as you will learn from the plethora of research I describe in this book, their healthy development may actually be compromised.

The Birth of *Raising Generation Tech*

The idea for *Raising Generation Tech* emerged at a confluence of several aspects of my life. As the author of three parenting books, I regularly counsel parents on how to help their children develop into healthy, happy, and successful people. I also work with kids to help them find their way through the complicated maze that we know as twenty-first-century childhood.

As a frequent writer and speaker on the role of technology in our lives, I'm acutely aware of the nexus between technology and family, and I offer ideas to my audiences on how they can best leverage technology to their family's advantage. As someone who is personally and professionally immersed in this technology, whether it be computers, mobile phones, the Internet, or social media, I have directly observed the influence that it has had on me, both positively and negatively, as a wholly assimilated digital immigrant.

Most important, as the father of two children who are growing up in this crazy new world, I have deep concerns about the role that popular culture and technology can play in their development. I want to ensure that this influence only contributes to my children's healthy growth. As a result, *Raising Generation Tech* isn't just an academic exercise of sharing my professional expertise and experience with you. Nor is this book about detailing the burgeoning body of research on the impact of popular culture and technology on children. More deeply, this book is a personal and family journey that my wife, Sarah, and I, like other couples, must navigate. This new world contains a cultural and technological landscape that is exciting, scary, and still largely uncharted. Like all parents, we must educate ourselves on this wired world in which our girls are digital natives and will lead lives thoroughly steeped in technology. We must make deliberate and sometimes tough decisions based on what we value, what we believe, what we have experienced, and what we have learned. This book is as much a shared process of awareness, discovery, understanding, and action with you as it is a guide on how to prepare children to survive and thrive in this crazy new world of popular culture and technology.

What Lies Ahead

Raising Generation Tech isn't a comprehensive encyclopedia of all things related to popular culture, technology, and children. Such a project could conceivably fill several volumes. In addition, there are many topics—such as television viewing, video-game violence, sexting, and cyberbullying— that have been addressed with great breadth and depth in more focused venues, such as other books, websites, newsletters, and blogs. An Internet search on many specific topics will reveal a wealth of useful information.

Instead, *Raising Generation Tech* focuses on issues that have a direct and practical relevance to the in-the-trenches parenting you do every day, for example, the values that children get from watching television, the seeming addiction that many children have to their technology, and the physical health risks of too much screen time. These issues may not be fully on your radar as consequential influences on your children because they are so woven into your family's lives and because they have a subtle and delayed impact.

Raising Generation Tech explores issues that are at the nexus of popular culture, technology, and children by looking at what the current research indicates and at what my professional and parenting experience has shown to be pertinent. In this book, we'll examine what we know now about popular culture, technology, and children, and then we'll gaze into a crystal ball to determine what we need to know in the coming years of your children's lives.

My fundamental goal in writing this book is twofold: to help you protect and then prepare your children for this crazy new world. First, I want to motivate and educate you to protect your children from the toxic aspects of popular culture and technology until they have the maturity and capabilities to use the wonderful benefits of those things to their advantage. Think of it this way: you establish boundaries to ensure your children's physical well-being because, for example, the risks of their running into the street are real and the consequences are immediate and potentially tragic. You should apply the same reasoning to when your children are, metaphorically speaking, at risk of running into the streets of popular culture and technology, because the possible harm, though less immediate, is no less significant. As a consequence, you must set appropriate limits on your children's experiences in this always-connected world to protect their psychological, emotional, intellectual, and social well-being.

Second, you can't protect your children forever; at some point, they will venture out into that crazy new world on their own. The question is whether you send them out ill equipped to survive or well prepared to thrive in this sometimes overwhelming world. I want to help you prepare your children for this digital world by instilling in them the values, attitudes, knowledge, and skills that will enable them to gain their benefits while avoiding their pitfalls. In summary, perhaps the most important goal of *Raising Generation Tech* is to offer you the information, insights, and tools you need to protect and prepare your children for this crazy new world of popular culture and technology.

I wrote this book to help you channel all of the positives that popular culture and technology have to offer your children while also helping you to mitigate the negatives, both obvious and hidden, that exist. The book begins by opening your eyes to the sometimes shocking presence of popular culture and technology in your children's lives. I don't use the word *shocking* lightly, but that was the word that best described what I felt when I began exploring the research on how and how much young people are using popular culture and technology today.

Part 1 of *Raising Generation Tech*, "That Crazy New World," educates you about the presence and importance of popular culture and technology in your children's lives. In chapter 1, you learn about the growing and oftentimes unhealthy influence that popular culture has over them. Chapter 2 details how much time children devote to technology, on what areas they are focused, and what specific aspects of it they are most involved in. Chapter 3 describes why it is essential that you instill healthy "defaults" in your children that will help you protect and prepare them for the popular culture and technology to which they will be exposed. And chapter 4 offers you my perspective on the kind of life that will enable your children to thrive in this crazy new world.

In Part 2, "Protect and Prepare Your Children," chapters 5–10 look at the six areas that I believe are most affected by popular culture and technology: self-identity, values, thinking, relationships, health, and life. These chapters offer in-depth discussions of the latest research and practical suggestions on how you can ensure that these areas are allowed to be fully developed, and not hindered by, your children's exposure to popular culture and technology.

Part 3, "The Hard Work and the Payoff," focuses on more practical ways that you can protect and prepare your children for a life immersed in popular culture and technology. Chapter 11 emphasizes the need to do the job you signed on for, namely being a parent, and to avoid being expedient with your children and taking the path of least resistance. Finally, Chapter 12 describes who Kids 3.0 are and who you want your children to become in preparation for this crazy new world of popular culture and technology.

This Is Urgent!

It's hard enough these days for parents to keep up with the latest popular cultural influences and technological developments. It's downright exhausting to stay attuned to what popular culture and technology are on our children's radars and what effect both are having on them. It's nigh impossible to be able to separate the healthy from the unhealthy influences.

Yet we must look long and hard at the relationships that our children are developing with popular culture and the torrent of technology available to them. This juncture in our society's history is critical because, given the unrelenting omnipresence of popular culture and the rapid pace of technological change, we simply can't know how these wide-ranging influences and changes will affect our children or our society.

The Chicken Littles of this crazy new world fear the recent and impending technological advancements and believe that the sky will fall if these developments continue. This fatalistic attitude, if you buy into it, will only serve to paralyze you and prevent you from confronting the rapidly changing landscape head-on. At the same time, despite their strident warnings, these alarmists don't actually have any practical suggestions on how to prevent this supposed Armageddon. As I noted earlier, you can't stop or control popular culture or technology, and you can't readily decouple your children (or yourselves) from the "matrix"—nor would you want to. All you can do is make informed decisions and take appropriate action in the best interests of your children.

To bury our heads in the sand would be irresponsible at best and catastrophic at worst. We must recognize that there are heightened dangers and heightened opportunities in all that this crazy new world offers. If we get this wrong, we could very well live in a world of zombies who used to be our children!

But seriously, without closely scrutinizing the impact of popular culture and technology on our children, we could be exposing them to a variety of threats, including cyberbullying, sexting, inappropriate content, privacy concerns, sexual predators, and manipulative advertisements. Here's a striking example: research shows that 90 percent of children between the ages of eight and sixteen have, often unintentionally, viewed pornography on the Internet, and one-third of sixteen- and seventeen-year-old boys watch online pornography regularly. How, for example, will young men's attitudes toward women and sexuality change now that pornography is so readily available?

At the same time, this crazy new world of popular culture and technology is teeming with incredible opportunities. Social media, for example, offers children prospects for increased individual and collaborative creativity, social connections, community involvement, exposure to diverse people, new learning experiences, and the development of essential technological skills. Just imagine who the superhumans of the future will be. If we can understand and shape popular culture and harness the amazing technology that lies at our children's fingertips—while ensuring that they're used as plowshares and not swords—we give our children the chance to become those superhumans who will flourish as we move deeper into the twenty-first century.

This leaves several difficult questions that we as parents must ask: Can we tease out the benefits that popular culture and technology have to offer while protecting our children from their harmful influences? Can we really understand and consciously manage the technology our children will be immersed in while balancing other academic, physical, artistic, and spiritual activities? If your answer is, "Yes, I can, and yes, I will!" then your efforts will result in raising Kids 3.0. That, I dare say, is a gift that keeps on giving. If, however, your answer is "No, I can't" or "I'm not sure," then you are potentially opening your children up to a world for which they will be overwhelmed and unprepared.

Payoff of Raising Kids 3.0

Raising Generation Tech is not intended to offer you a Chicken Little view of popular culture and technology or to cause you to fear for your children's lives as they become uploaded, metaphorically speaking, into cyberspace. To the contrary, my intention is to inform you about all that popular culture and technology have to offer—the good, the bad, and the ugly. I hope to provide you with the knowledge, insights, perspectives, and practical tools that will empower you to make informed decisions about your children's use of popular culture and technology in ways that maximize its benefits and minimize its potential harm.

The payoff for raising Kids 3.0 is immense. First, you'll educate your children about popular culture and technology so they see these things for what they are, namely tools that enhance their lives rather than forces that define them. Second, you'll raise your children protected from these influences until they are fully prepared to use them wisely. Third, your children will be masters, instead of victims, thus enabling them to enjoy these tools to their fullest benefit while avoiding their many hazards. The ultimate payoff is for your children to develop into value-driven, happy, successful, and connected people (in the old-school sense) while also enjoying all that popular culture has to offer and gaining an appreciation for and becoming sufficiently skilled at using the technology that will come to play such a central role in their lives.

Part I

This Crazy New World

Chapter 1

Popular Culture Today

Survey results of children younger than 10: What do you think is the very best thing in the world?

1. *Being a celebrity*
2. *Good looks*
3. *Being rich*
4. *Being healthy*
5. *Pop music*
6. *Families*
7. *Friends*
8. *Nice food*
9. *Watching films*
10. *Heaven and/or God*

Popular culture may be the most powerful force in your children's lives today, and regrettably, the preponderance of research suggests that its influence is more negative than positive—and many parents agree. In a recent survey, three-fourths of parents believed that materialism and the negative influences from television, movies, and music were a "serious problem" in raising children. More than 85 percent of parents believed that marketing contributes to children being too materialistic, that sexual content in media leads children to become sexually active at a younger age, and that violent content increases aggressive behavior in children. Nevertheless, 66 percent of parents think that they could do a better job of supervising their children's media exposure.

Despite this influence, many parents don't fully understand precisely what popular culture is or how it affects their children. When I ask groups of parents what popular culture is, they usually say things like *American Idol*, Kim Kardashian, McDonald's, Kanye West, and LeBron James. This list only gives examples of popular culture. These are, if you will, some expressions of popular culture, but they don't really tell us what popular culture is.

The typical sociological view is that popular culture is the collection of popular icons, heroes and heroines, and rituals, myths, and beliefs that express our society's values. When a critical mass of people adopts certain values, attitudes, beliefs, and interests, those things become the accepted norm that shapes the cultural thinking, decisions, and direction in which a culture goes. Popular culture was then expressed and disseminated through the limited forms of media that existed before the Internet revolution, for example, television, radio, and print.

The formation of this popular culture was vital to a healthy and vibrant society, and it provided citizens with continuity and predictability. At the same time, it offered children a coherent picture, one that made sense to them, of how society worked. This popular culture conveyed to children the notions of what it would take to succeed in society.

Oh, how times have changed! I would argue that, coincidental with the rise of technology, the current popular culture—or what I more accurately call synthetic culture—now dictates rather than reflects the present cultural zeitgeist. Popular culture, through its conduits of modern technology, old school (e.g., movies, television, radio, magazines), recent school (e.g., video games, DVDs), and new school (e.g., the Internet, mobile phones, social media), is omnipresent, intense, and unrelenting in its ability to send messages to children. I don't think it is a stretch to suggest that many of popular culture's messages are unhealthy. In fact, popular culture has become a voracious beast of materialism, celebrity, and excess that shapes values to meet its own greedy needs. Many heroes offered by popular culture are not heroic (e.g., Kanye West); many of its icons represent unhealthy values (e.g., the Kardashians); and many of its rituals, myths, and beliefs (e.g., consumerism, wealth will bring happiness, success at any cost) are in its own best interests, not those of your children.

Not All Popular Culture Is Bad

I'm not suggesting that all popular culture is bad. To the contrary, I believe it is neither good nor bad, neither a tool nor a weapon. What makes popular culture go one way or the other depends on how you use it, the messages it's sending, and how you and your children respond to those messages. Popular culture can be a wonderful outlet for entertainment and escapism. Whether film, television, video games, music, or sports, activities that transport us from our daily lives into temporary alternative realities can play healthy roles in our lives. These diversions act as brief respites from our otherwise busy lives and give us a time-out that relieves stress, creates pleasant vicarious emotions, and just plain entertains us. As long as the messages communicated in the media aren't bad for children, who am I to say that Federico Fellini is better than Judd Apatow or that Beethoven is better than Lady Gaga.

Nevertheless, let's be clear here: even "good" popular culture isn't that good for children. Although there are educational television programs, video games that encourage creativity and problem solving, and movies with positive messages, used in excess and without consideration, these media still teach children bad habits:

- Experience life vicariously instead of directly.
- Be sedentary rather than physically active.

- Have indirect social contact with others instead of real contact.
- Don't participate in activities that directly support intellectual, emotional, cultural, spiritual, and physical development.

Children as Consumers

Most harmfully, popular culture attempts to manipulate your children's needs and wants to motivate them to buy food, toys, clothing, electronics, and other products that have no redeeming value, are unhealthy, or send them the wrong messages. Popular culture is big business; $1.2 billion was spent in advertising in 2010, a double-digit increase over 2009. Research has also shown that children significantly influence their family's food and drink purchases, which, nationally, total $100 billion each year, much of which goes toward unhealthy foods.

The line between entertainment and advertising is becoming increasingly blurred. For example, the toy manufacturer Hasbro has a 50 percent ownership stake in the Hub, a children's television network that was launched in 2010. Commercials aside, this channel's programming is basically a direct-marketing platform for selling Hasbro toys. In addition, recent technological advances have enabled companies that market to children to create "supersystems" around their brands that incorporate 360-degree multimedia universes devoted exclusively to selling their products. These supersystems include television shows, websites, YouTube videos, fan clubs, Facebook pages, Twitter feeds, and video games, as well as traditional advertising.

The advertising industry is also leveraging the Web to attract children. Children's food, drink, and toy manufacturers, including Disney and Nabisco, are using websites, online games, and mobile phone apps to connect children to their products without traditional advertising. In effect, these media are providing product advertisements wrapped in the guise of entertainment and fun. Children become unwitting marketers by sharing these forms of "entertainment" with their peers through texting and social media.

These arguments against much of what popular culture has to offer are not just my opinion or anecdotal evidence; they are supported by research. For example, one study found that children who watched more movies and television and played more video games asked for more toys, food, and beverages. As one of the researchers pointed out, "Younger children aren't even able to understand that ads, which are now cropping up in video games and movies, online and even in mobile phones, are intended to sell them things." The number of ads that children are exposed to is mind boggling; the average child sees or hears around forty thousand advertisements each year (and about one million by the time he or she turns twenty-one years old), which primarily sell sugary breakfast cereal, salty snacks, fast food, candy, and toys.

The explosive growth of video games has been nothing less than staggering. Sales of video games topped 220 million, worth $18 billion, in 2010, and 65 percent of households with children own a video-game system. Surveys estimate that 80 percent of the most popular video games have violent themes, and 50 percent of video games that were chosen as favorites by fourth- through eighth-grade children had violent content. A survey of video-game use found that, of 118 M-rated games (for mature audiences, older than age seventeen), 70 percent were targeted at children younger than seventeen years of age. Particularly troublesome is that unaccompanied children between thirteen and sixteen years old were able to buy M-rated video games 85 percent of the time. These findings are no small matter, because studies have shown that children who play violent video games, particularly boys, are more likely to exhibit increased aggressive thinking, emotions, and behavior, as well as delin-quency. Research has also reported that academic achievement is nega-tively related to the amount of time spent playing video games. What's more, these violent video games commonly portray gender stereotypes of women as helpless and sexually provocative.

The Sexualization of Girls

The sexualization of young girls is also on the rise. For example, take a look at the marketing tactics used to sell the Monster High line of dolls from Mattel—dolls that seem pretty darned inappropriate for girls as young as six years old. Some of these dolls' descriptions include, "Favorite activity: shopping and flirting with boys!...I'm also gorgeous, intimidating...I like to show up to parties in my scary little black dress... Readying myself for public adoration...My friends say I have the perfect figure for fashion." They also look like little prostitutes (in my opinion). Fascinatingly, parents' reviews on Amazon.com are uniformly adulatory: parents and girls love these dolls! Here's the kicker: the only negative reviews are related to the quality of the dolls (e.g., arms and legs falling off), with very few comments related to the dolls' sexual nature. As the father of two girls, I am acutely aware of and concerned about—OK, shocked by—these messages from popular culture and the parents who think that these dolls are appropriate for young girls (or girls of any age, for that matter).

The expectations of young girls to look sexy go up once they hit their tween years. The use of makeup (e.g., mascara, eyeliner, lipstick) among eight- to twelve-year-old girls, for example, has increased dra-matically in recent years. Who is supporting this trend? Sadly, the answer is parents, with 66 percent of surveyed girls saying that a family member helped them buy and apply the makeup. Another influence is actresses who star in teen-oriented shows, for example, Selena Gomez and Miley Cyrus (who are both, in fact, nearly twenty) and appear heavily made up. Cosmetic lines by these teen stars are also culprits.

Your Children Know about Popular Culture

I've spoken to tens of thousands of children and teens over the years—from five years old up to high school seniors—and have learned something surprising: most children aren't fooled by popular culture. They know a lot of it is bad. They know that all popular culture cares about is making money. They know that the messages it communicates are unhealthy. Most children also know the difference between good and bad values and right and wrong. At the same time, they lack the experience, perspective, and tools to avoid succumbing to popular culture's attraction: its bells and whistles, its bright lights and loud music, its beautiful people. Children are simply overwhelmed by popular culture's force, and that force has grown significantly with each new form of technology.

The Relationship of Kids 3.0 with Popular Culture

You can't protect your children from the corrosive aspects of popular culture forever; sooner or later, they will have to confront this crazy new world on their own. If you want your children to become true Kids 3.0 who are prepared to thrive in this world, they need to develop a healthy relationship with popular culture that allows them to enjoy what it has to offer while at the same time being wary of its dark side.

When you educate your children about the positive and negative aspects of popular culture, you give them the opportunity—and the power—to approach its growing influence in their lives from a position of strength. You want your children to have control over their engagement with popular culture and the wherewithal to see both its benefits and risks. They can then make deliberate choices about the quality and quantity of popular culture in which they wish to immerse themselves.

To build this positive relationship with popular culture, given its omnipresence and intensity, you must be proactive in giving your children the values, attitudes, and skills to keep popular culture in its proper place. Children will inevitably be exposed to popular culture, but when you give them the right tools to form a positive relationship with it, you can be confident that your children will develop into Kids 3.0 who are prepared to keep popular culture in perspective and use it as a tool for their entertainment and enjoyment rather than as a weapon that hurts them.

Raising Kids 3.0: Know Popular Culture

- Keep a journal of your children's popular culture intake and their other activities (e.g., homework, extracurricular activities, time with friends and family) for a week.

- Judge whether your children's use of popular culture is in balance with their other activities.

- Test your knowledge of your children's popular culture activities.

- Identify the healthy and unhealthy messages your children get from popular culture.

- Ask yourself whether those messages are consistent with the values, beliefs, and attitudes you want your children to learn.

- Consider making changes on the basis of what you've learned.

Chapter 2

Technology Today

"You might be surprised to learn that I, as an eighth grader, found myself in full agreement…on social networking. I don't enjoy social networking, because I feel it detracts from my 'real' relationships. I have never had an interesting conversation over social networking. Without a computer, I would be forced to read a book (or the Times*), but social networking almost always presents an excusable distraction. Often when I try to have an in-person conversation with someone about a real-world event, they are looking at a screen, their mind somewhere else, and even as they are eternally 'connected,' I can feel them drifting away from me. There is so much to not focus on in cyberspace that while we are endlessly available, we are seldom present."*

—Lily, thirteen years old

Before you can begin to understand the impact of technology on your children and how technological advances will influence them in the future, we should first look at how we've arrived at this point in history at which there may be no more powerful force in their lives. I've always found that looking back to where we came from can help us better understand where we are today and, more important, where we may be going in the years ahead.

The Past

So, let's consider the history of communications technology. When we think about such technology, we usually think of gadgets made of silicon chips and circuit boards. But technology has been in existence for as long as humans have walked the earth, although its earlier forms—though cutting edge at the time—were obviously rather primitive and unsophisticated from our perspective today.

We officially became *Homo sapiens* approximately two hundred thousand years ago. With the emergence of spoken language (the first form of social media, I might add), we were able to communicate with one another face-to-face, which allowed for the emergence of civilization as we know it. Of course, this connection was limited to, well, a shouting distance, but it was a start. After the development of spoken language, there were virtually no advances in communication technology for another 196,000 years.

About 4,000 years ago, humans developed their first means of non-face-to-face communication with the discovery of smoke signals and then, about 2,500 years ago, drums. For the first time, people were able to connect without being in physical proximity to one another. This development allowed diverse people to connect and groups to extend their reach beyond their immediate surroundings. But early advances, unlike today, were few and far between; not much changed in communication technology for about 2,300 years.

The discovery and production of electricity by Benjamin Franklin in 1752 and Alessandro Volta in 1800, respectively, opened a door to a new era characterized by rapid and dramatic technological developments. Around 1835, Samuel Morse invented the telegraph, setting the stage for the greatest period of technological advancement in history, which, in a relatively short period of time, created an impact that continues to touch our lives today. Think about it: the telegraph was a clear precursor to the Internet, and the telegram was an early iteration of email.

Alexander Graham Bell's patent of the telephone in 1876 (many have laid claim to having actually invented it) enabled humans to converse directly in real time over great distances as if they were in the same room. The world got smaller (metaphorically speaking, of course).

The facsimile followed closely in the wake of the telephone, paving the way for the immediate transmission of something other than voice. For the first time, documents could be shared at a rate far faster than through the traditional mail (what we now quaintly refer to as snail mail).

Mobile phone technology emerged for commercial use with the car phone around 1979 and the first truly handheld device in 1983. The mobile phone has progressively evolved to its present state: small, able to perform a multitude of functions, ubiquitous, and an indispensible part of our lives.

In 1994, the Internet was introduced to the public (it had actually been around since the 1960s in the military and in universities), and it has likely been the single greatest leap forward in communications technology, as it enables the instantaneous transmission of voice, data, documents, and still and moving images. It has created a veritable deluge of technology in fewer than two decades: the Web, email, text messaging, and an array of applications—from MySpace, Facebook, and YouTube to Twitter and Skype—that have dramatically altered the way we live, work, relate to others, and much, much more.

This brief, and admittedly incomplete, history may not be news to you, but it provides a little perspective on how we arrived at the present in terms of technology and how these developments have changed the way we view and interact with our world. It may bring to light how technology may influence us, both positively and negatively, and how we will adapt to such developments in the future.

What Has Changed

What do all these communication technologies have in common? They have incrementally enabled us to connect with more people and access more information in faster, easier, and more cost-efficient ways. Each advancement changed our lives in ways manifest and subtle, direct and indirect, predictable and unexpected. Modern technology may be the most powerful tool in our lives today, with personal, informational, economic, social, cultural, and political impacts.

What lies at the heart of this evolution is the way we perceive time, distance, and relationships. Each iteration of this technology has involved a shift in how we experience time and distance and how each influences us. Time has shrunk as communication has become instantaneous. Distance also seems to have grown shorter as we are able to connect with people at the far corners of the earth. We are no longer bound by our physical limitations. Our relationships, because of the changes in time and distance, are no longer limited to people in our immediate surroundings. We are able to connect to and build relationships with people as many and diverse as there are countries in the world.

Our expectations of time, distance, and relationships have changed. These changed expectations, in turn, circle back to alter our relationship with technology. Before the Internet, mobile phones, text messaging, and Twitter, we simply knew we couldn't be reached readily by anyone except in person or by landline telephone. Being disconnected was the norm. We were comfortable with being disconnected, and any ability to connect to others was a bonus.

These days, the expectation is that we can be connected in numerous ways with anyone at any time and instantaneously. Our default is connectivity, so being connected has become the norm and our comfort zone. Any break from that norm—caused by the loss of Internet connection, the absence of a cellular signal, or simply forgetting our mobile phones at home—takes us out of that comfort zone and, as recent research has found, can create real feelings of loss, anxiety, and panic.

Technology Today

Shock is the best word I can think of to describe my reaction to the results of the latest Kaiser Foundation survey of technology use by young people ages eight to eighteen. The 2009 study was a follow-up to an identical survey the foundation conducted in 2005. In the previous survey, the researchers found that, on average, young people spent more than five and a half hours a day interacting with technology unrelated to school. At the time, the researchers assumed that, given young people's busy schedules, an increase in their use of technology was impossible. How wrong they were!

The latest survey revealed that in 2009, this same age group spent more than seven and a half hours a day involved with non-school-related technology. That's an increase of more than one-third in just four years! Speaking of shocked, the researchers themselves were astounded at the increase; between school, homework, extracurricular activities, socializing, eating, sleeping, and family time, there simply didn't seem to be enough time in a day. When the time when young people were multitasking was counted separately—for example, when a teenager was watching TV, writing a paper on his laptop, and having text-message conversations for twenty minutes, which would add up to sixty minutes of total technology use—the total time immersed in technology rose to ten and three-quarter hours. That didn't even include the use of technology for school.

Let's look at what specific technology consumed so much of the young people's time: television: 4:29 hours; computer: 2:31 hours; video games: 1:13 hours; and movies: 0:25 hours. (There was some good news; respondents spent 0:28 hours a day reading—reading isn't dead yet!) Of the time spent on a computer, social networking accounted for 25 percent, playing games accounted for 19 percent, video sites counted for 16 percent, and instant messaging for 13 percent. I found it surprising that, despite being so twentieth century, the idiot box (aka the television) is still much beloved and used by this generation. The survey revealed that 64 percent of families watched TV during meals, 45 percent of families left on the TV when no one was watching, and remarkably 71 percent of children had TVs in their bedrooms.

Other research has found that 97 percent of children between the ages of twelve and seventeen play video games. Contrary to the popular perception that video games are a solitary pursuit, almost two-thirds play video games with family and friends, and more than one-fourth play with people on the Internet. Here's an eye-opening statistic: the average young person spends up to ten thousand hours playing video and online games by the age of twenty-one. That's about the same amount of time they devote to their middle and high school years!

The research also reported that almost a quarter of teenagers access social media sites at least ten times a day, and more than 50 percent use social media once a day. In addition, 75 percent of teens own mobile phones (up from 45 percent in 2004), and texting was a dominant form of communication for children and teens, with girls sending eighty text messages a day and boys sending thirty a day on average. Fifty-nine percent of girls text their friends many times a day "just to say hello." One girl sent more than two thousand messages in one day. In addition, 83 percent take photos, and 64 percent share those photos with their friends using social media. Finally, 50 percent of the teenagers with driver's licenses indicated that they sent and read text messages while they were driving.

The impact of technology on studying and grades was significant. Thirty-one percent of children said that they multitasked while doing their homework most of the time, and another quarter indicated they did so 25 percent of the time. This despite a growing body of evidence (discussed in chapter 7) that proves that multitasking interferes with learning. Additionally, 66 percent of light technology users reported good grades and only 23 percent indicated fair or poor grades. With moderate use, the percentage with good grades stayed about the same (65 percent), but there was a substantial increase in the percentage of students with fair or poor grades (31 percent). The effect of heavy use of technology was even more pronounced, with only 51 percent of heavy users reporting good grades and 47 percent indicating fair or poor grades.

How much has technology taken over the lives of children and their parents' priorities today? A study by AVG, an Internet security company, found that young children are more likely to master tech skills than life skills. For example, although 58 percent of two- to five-year-olds can play a computer game, only 43 percent can ride a bike. Of children in that age group, 10 percent can use a smartphone application, whereas only 9 percent can tie their shoes. Here's a scary statistic: more young children can open a web browser than can swim.

The Parent-Child Disconnect

What is clear in this new technological landscape is that parents and children see technology in vastly different ways. For example, one study found that parents were two to three times more likely (72–88 percent) than their children (17–35 percent) to be concerned about social isolation, Internet addiction, lack of physical activity, and posting and viewing sexual content. A similar disconnect between parents (12–34 percent) and children (8–16 percent) was found for whether social media interfered with children's offline activities, including schoolwork, family time, outdoor activities, offline friendships, and chores.

Another disconnect was found between the concerns that parents and children have about the presence of sexual predators online. Parents were two and a half times more likely to be concerned about online predators than their children were (fewer than 10 percent of children reported having experienced "uncomfortable" sexual situations online).

Nevertheless, attesting to parents' naïveté or ignorance of their children's use of technology, there was yet another disconnect between parents' concerns and their responses to those concerns. For example, in one study, just over a third of parents had never visited their children's social media pages, and 43 percent weren't sure how much time their children spent online each week. Of the parents who said they knew how often their children were online, their estimates significantly underestimated the actual time their children spent online.

Also, the amount of time that parents devoted to monitoring their children's online activities declined steadily from less than 30 percent of parents with children in their early teens to only 13 percent of parents with children who were in their later teens. This drop in attentiveness runs contrary to the evidence that older children are more likely to be using technology in unhealthy ways.

Researchers in one study asked children whether their parents had rules governing their use of different forms of technology. In most categories, most children said no: television, 68 percent; computers, 60 percent; video games, 66 percent; and music, 85 percent. To highlight still another disconnect, when asked whether parents set limits on their children's Internet and social media use, 46 percent of parents said they set limits, but only 36 percent of children confirmed those limits. So who are we to believe? In either case, those numbers are alarmingly low, particularly given the strength of the concerns that so many parents expressed. This study suggested that the lack of meaningful action in response to these concerns was due to the presence of computers in 50 percent of children's rooms and the fact that 55 percent of parents believed that social media was just a passing Internet fad. The bottom line is that the majority of parents don't keep an eye on or set limits on their children's use of technology.

Lost Opportunities

Another point I want to make is that when children are engaged in technology, whether watching television or a movie, using social networking sites, or playing online games, they are incurring opportunity costs. Opportunity cost is an economics concept, but in this context, it can refer to the idea that when children devote time to one area (in this case, technology), the cost is the value that would have been gained had they devoted that time to another area.

So the substantial commitment of time and energy to technology has two costs. First, the excessive or inappropriate use of technology can harm your children psychologically, emotionally, intellectually, physically, neurologically, and socially. The second cost is the potential benefits that children might have accrued if they had directed that time and energy to other, possibly healthier, activities. So, as you weigh the frequency and content of the technology you allow your children to be exposed to, you should add opportunity costs to the equation.

The Law of Unintended Consequences

Let's not forget that technology is not an end in itself but rather a means to an end. What should that end be? Enhancing the quality of our children's lives and fostering their fullest development, hopefully. Yet can we say unequivocally that the latest technology is doing that? As the evidence I present in *Raising Generation Tech* attests, the answer is clearly no. As a result, it's our responsibility as parents to ensure that the technology our children are exposed to is well understood and that they take full advantage of its many benefits while reducing its potential costs.

We can see the law of unintended consequences everywhere in our technological lives. Consider the Internet, mobile phones, texting, Facebook, and Twitter. Here's a satirical and fictitious quote from the website of the *Onion*, attributed to Twitter cofounder Jack Dorsey about his invention: "Twitter was intended to be a way for vacant, self-absorbed egotists to share their most banal and idiotic thoughts with anyone pathetic enough to read them. When I heard how Iranians were using my beloved creation for their own means—such as organizing a political movement and informing the outside world of the actions of a repressive regime—I couldn't believe they'd ruined something so beautiful, simple, and absolutely pointless."

Though Dorsey was speaking, fictionally, with tongue firmly planted in cheek, who would have predicted that Twitter would play a key role in the election of a president or the promotion of freedom in countries such as China and Iran? At the same time, who would have thought that mobile phones would be used as a high-tech form of bullying or that drivers who text are twenty-three times more likely to get into an accident? It's still far too early in the evolution of technology to know what its impact on children will be. Of course, we can never know a priori all the unintended consequences of any new technology, but reducing the consequences could make the positive effects of new technology all the more beneficial and its negative effects more manageable and less destructive.

Yes, let us continue to nurture emerging technology to further leverage all that it has to offer. But the journey of progress should be guided by us, not led by the technology itself. To do otherwise would be to take the risk of technology leading us down a road of unintended consequences rather than a road of our choosing.

Cautionary Tales

The statistics I've just presented should be disturbing to you. They clearly demonstrate the staggering amount of time that young people devote to technology. At the same time, the data don't directly explore how technology is positively and negatively affecting young people, nor do they adequately represent the human side of this interaction between technology and children. A 2010 *New York Times* article, however, does humanize this data, highlighting stories about young people's use of technology and how it affects their lives, families, and futures. Out of respect for the privacy of the students I discuss, I'm not naming names—though, incredibly, these young people and their parents allowed themselves to be identified in the *Times* article.

A school in the heart of Silicon Valley, the birthplace and epicenter of technology, moved the start of the day an hour later to accommodate students who are staying up later, ostensibly because they spend so much time online at the expense of their schoolwork and their health.

A high school senior with a passion for filmmaking devoted so much time and energy to technology that its presence had turned into a counterproductive force to both his present life and his future goals. For instance, he regularly neglects his schoolwork to work on his video projects. He plays video games ten hours a week and updates his Facebook page in the wee hours of the morning. The results of this absorption in technology include poor grades and concerns about his getting into the college of his choice to pursue his love of filmmaking.

This next example is nothing less than mind boggling. A fourteen-year-old girl sends up to twenty-seven thousand text messages a month. No, that was not a typo: twenty-seven thousand. I did the math, and it seems inconceivable. Assuming that this girl is awake eighteen hours a day (which means that she's not getting enough sleep), she is sending fifty texts an hour or almost one text a minute. The girl indicated that she usually carries on multiple text conservations at once (which is obviously the only way this math could work out). How does she have time to do anything else, such as eat, study, or actually talk to other people? Gosh, I hope her family has an unlimited texting plan!

Another boy plays video games six hours a day during the week and even more on weekends. Let's do some more math. After you subtract the six hours this boy devotes to video games, assuming that he is in school eight hours a day (including transportation and transitions from one activity to another) and sleeps eight hours at night, that leaves two hours each day to study, eat, participate in extracurricular activities, and interact with actual human beings.

So what, or should I say *who*, is missing from these stories? If you said parents, you hit the nail right on the head. Where, for the love of all things sacred, are the parents? Largely in absentia apparently, despite the obvious harm that their children's obsession with technology is inflicting on their lives.

According to the *Times* article, parents seem to fall into several categories. First, there are the parents who work full-time and simply aren't around to monitor and limit their children's use of technology. Research shows that these parents tend to earn a lower income, and their children's use of technology actually hurts them academically, contrary to the popular belief that owning a computer is beneficial to children academically.

Other parents just seem to be in denial. One father stated that if children aren't up on technology, they're going to fall behind—even though his son's grades have slipped and the boy admits that he hasn't exercised in several years.

Still others are veritable Luddites who seem incapable of or unwilling to understand the connected world that their children inhabit. They indicate that they just don't know enough about technology to gain control of their children's digital habits. I would suggest that, given the potential consequences, ignorance isn't an excuse for neglecting what's best for children.

The final category is what I call capitulating parents, who actually enable their children's unhealthy relationship with technology. For example, the parents of the young filmmaker I previously discussed bought him a state-of-the-art, $2,000 computer so he could pursue his dream. These parents are also rationalizers; the boy's mother tried to convince herself that it was the right decision by saying that her son was really making an effort to do his homework. In fact, his grades did initially improve, mostly because he was taking a lighter course load and avoiding advanced classes, but then they declined again as he was neglecting his schoolwork because—you guessed it—he was spending time on his brand-spanking-new computer instead of studying.

Several of the students interviewed in the article recognized that their use of technology was out of hand and that they couldn't control themselves, and they actually wished that their parents would step in and set limits. Yet their parents still didn't take action.

So who's responsible here? I can't blame these children, because they lack the maturity to make good decisions, and they're just living in the world they were born into. So who's left? Their parents, of course, who have abdicated their essential role as, well, parents. They have failed to establish expectations, set limits, and administer consequences, thereby putting their children's health and well-being at risk. Parents' job is to set boundaries, plain and simple. I'm just amazed that so many parents, who obviously love their children, are well intentioned, and want what's best for their children, aren't up to the task when it comes to technology.

But, because you are reading this book, you have put yourself into a different category of parents. You recognize the concerns and potential risks associated with your children having excessive and unguided immersion in technology. You also see the need to consciously shape and guide and limit your children's use of technology. To you I say, "Bravo!"

Your Family's Relationship with Technology

The research I have presented here gives a persuasive sense of the average young person's relationship with technology. But your children may not be average; they may be more or less involved with technology. In addition, as the research and cautionary tales here illustrate, your children's degree of involvement in technology only partially determines its impact on them. How savvy you are in your understanding and use of technology also determines that impact.

So here's an exercise for you. Over the course of a week or so, track how often your children use each form of technology. Use the statistics I've described to compare your children with others. If your children are within the typical range of technology use, you will probably be surprised—and maybe even shocked—at how much time they spend in the digital world.

So how did your children develop their relationship with technology? In all likelihood, your relationship to technology had a major impact on the development of your children's relationship to technology. You influence your children's exposure to technology in two ways. First, whether consciously or otherwise, you determine the technology that your children are exposed to and how frequently they use it. You buy it for them, give them permission to use it, and provide them with the time and space for its use.

Second, and perhaps more important, you model the use of technology in your own life. When you use technology, you're constantly sending your children messages about the role that it should play in their lives. Think about your relationship with technology. How often do you, for example, watch television, play video games, surf the Internet, or check your email? In looking at your own relationship with technology, you may see the kind of relationship your children have or will develop with it.

To help you better understand how tech savvy you are and your own relationship with the connected world, take the exercise you just did for your children and apply it to yourself: what forms of technology do you use and how often? You may be surprised at how much time you devote to technology.

By gaining insights into the relationships that you and your children have with technology, you'll be able use the information in this book to help ensure that technology is a positive and healthy force in your family members' lives.

The Future

My concern is not with technology itself; we cannot and should not try to slow or halt the inexorable march of progress. My interest is in our children's relationship with that technology, and my concern is in how technology will affect them. Will they be passive recipients—dare I say victims?—of technology who allow it to change their lives for better or worse without consideration? Or can we teach our children to be masters of technology who deliberately harness its tremendous value while minimizing its risks?

The answers to these questions depend not only on the technology itself that is developed but also on our exploration of how new technology will influence our children's lives. Could anyone have predicted how

rapidly evolving communications technology would change the world
in which our children live? Well, in broad strokes, the scholar Marshall
McLuhan did foresee the future more than fifty years ago. For the sake of
future generations, we should continue to do so. Good questions to ask
include the following:

1. How do we hope our children will use this technology?
2. How will it affect their intellectual, educational, physical, social,
    moral, and spiritual development?
3. How will it affect our children's use of their time?
4. What benefit will it bring to our children?
5. What costs might arise from its use for our children?

The Relationship of Kids 3.0 with Technology

I hear many parents say that they're worried that their children won't be
tech savvy if they don't immerse them in technology early in their lives.
So, they put screens in front of their children from day 1, give them easy
access to technology early and often, and buy them iPads when they turn
four or five years old. Your children's competencies in the ins and outs of
technology are not the issue, though; you can be absolutely certain that
they will be competent with technology, because it is so omnipresent in
their lives. What is at issue is the relationship that your children develop
with technology—their attitude toward it and the role it plays in their
lives. It is this relationship that will determine whether your children
develop into Kids 3.0.

Unfortunately, as I discuss throughout this book, too many children
these days start off on the wrong foot with technology. Exposure that
is undirected and comes too early results in an unhealthy relationship,
one in which they see technology—whether computers, smartphones, or

social media—as an indelible part of who they are and in which its use is inextricably connected to how they feel about themselves.

It's easy for parents to give children gadgets to appease them or to occupy their time, but that won't necessarily prepare children for a healthy life in the digital world. As I mentioned earlier, most children today learn to use technology before they learn what used to be seminal life skills, such as tying shoes, riding bikes, and swimming. In addition, as I described earlier in this chapter, most children receive little guidance and few limits from their parents as to their use of technology.

We cannot expose our children to technology first and then give them guidance on its use after it's in their hands. Doing so is analogous to giving children a sharp knife without first teaching them how to use it safely; used properly, the knife is a tool, but without guidance, it can become a weapon. Plus, once a relationship based on unguided experience, attitudes, and habits is established between children and technology, there is little hope of reshaping that relationship in a more positive direction later on.

You shouldn't feel the need to rush your children into using technology because of the fear that they will be ill prepared to survive in the digital world. To the contrary, exposing them to technological experiences when they lack maturity only hurts them in the long run. In fact, I would argue that, to raise Kids 3.0, your priority early on in your children's lives should be to instill old-school values, attitudes, and skills in them rather than to expose them early to new-school ways created by technology.

By raising your children to be Kids 3.0, your children will gain several benefits. First, if you focus on what they need to develop into good, capable people (which takes a long time and a lot of effort), they will, in fact, become the good, capable people you want them to be (which is, I think you would agree, your most important goal). Second, you ensure that your children are prepared psychologically, emotionally, and socially to experience technology in a healthy way. Third, you demonstrate your (hopefully) positive relationship with and attitude toward technology, which they will likely take after. Finally, you have the time to educate your children about their use of technology so that they grow into informed and active captains, rather than uneducated and passive passengers, on the good ship USS *Technology*.

With the hard work of laying the foundation of raising good kids behind you (which, of course, is a job that is never *really* finished), you can comfortably and confidently immerse your children in the tech world at a later age. You can be confident of two things: first, they will acquire the necessary skills far more quickly than you could imagine. Second, your children, as Kids 3.0, will be better prepared to use technology responsibly as they proceed through childhood to adolescence and adulthood than are children who were handed technology right out of the womb (or so it seemed).

Showing your children how to develop a healthy relationship with technology begins with making a decision about what type of technology you expose your children to and how often they are permitted to use it at various stages of their development. This decision should be made in an informed and conscious fashion and should be based on your values, attitudes, and personal involvement with technology, as well as the latest research. As part of this process, you want to both model and discuss what a healthy relationship with technology is with your children and instill in them the values, attitudes, and skills that will further encourage them to develop a beneficial relationship with technology.

Part of this process involves paying attention not only to the content of the technology your children use—for example, the video games they play or the websites they visit—but also to the medium itself. As I quoted

Marshall McLuhan earlier ("The medium is the message"), we are often so focused on the content of technology that we don't consider how our children's simple interaction with it influences them. Yet this involvement in technology includes the specific ways in which children engage with it, for example, what they think, feel, and do as they are immersed in technology.

In summary, the goal is to raise Kids 3.0 who have a healthy perspective about the role of technology in their lives: technology is a tool to enhance their lives but is in no way a central part of who they are or how they feel about themselves. The relationship that Kids 3.0 have with technology is one of mastery rather than dependence, which enables them to take advantage of its many benefits while eschewing its more harmful elements.

Raising Kids 3.0: Know Technology

- Test your knowledge of your children's technology-related activities.

- Track your children's use of technology for a week and compare it with the data in this chapter.

- Track your own use of technology for a week and see if your own use seems reasonable or excessive.

- Identify the ways in which technology can benefit your children.

- Identify the ways in which technology can hurt your children.

- Consider making changes on the basis of what you've learned about your and your children's relationships with technology.

Chapter 3
Setting Defaults in Your Children

"I started to think about things to do without media and found out that actually I couldn't think of many."

—*Chilean college student*

I've always enjoyed the latest technology and consider myself an early adopter. For several years, I've been blogging on the impact of technology on people's personal and professional lives. One notion that is commonly used in the technology world is that of default, which, in computer speak, is a "preset option: an option that will automatically be selected by a computer if the user does not choose another alternative" (think of the font and margins that are set in Microsoft Word or the browser that always opens when you connect to the Internet). As I became increasingly immersed in both the technology and the parenting worlds, I came to see how defaults had considerable meaning and value in how children are raised.

You may think that computer terminology is a long way from parenthood. You may even be insulted by my equating things as cold and calculating as computers with the living, breathing incarnations of yourself. The reality is that children are programmed during the early years of their childhood to develop defaults. To apply the definition I provided in the previous paragraph to children, defaults are automatically selected by children if they do not deliberately choose another option. That is to say, your children's defaults, which are based on previous life experiences, are their immediate reactions to life circumstances, their initial thoughts, emotions, decisions, and actions in any given situation. Defaults are so influential because children will almost always use the first option that arrives in their outbox when faced with any given situation. The question is whether you want to be the one deciding what those defaults are or whether you want to entrust popular culture and technology with that responsibility. By installing positive defaults in your children, they are more likely to select healthy options over harmful alternatives.

The Power of Defaults

Defaults are so important for children for several reasons. The cognitive sciences have shown that people attempt to maximize their efficiency by choosing the most readily available courses of action. Whatever means that allow children to act with the least amount of cognitive processing will usually be the path they choose. The defaults that are instilled in your children at an early age act as that efficient mechanism.

Also, a growing body of neurological research has demonstrated that the prefrontal cortex, the part of the brain associated with so-called executive functioning, such as impulse control, risk-reward comparisons, future planning, and decision making, isn't fully developed until young adults are in their early twenties. This finding has important implications for defaults. Without well-ingrained defaults that trigger positive behavior, children have a greater chance of acting without sufficient thought and are more easily influenced by less-than-healthy forces, such as popular culture. The bottom line is that the defaults that become ingrained early in children's lives, whether healthy or otherwise, will, to a great extent, determine their behavior in the future.

How Defaults Develop

Children develop defaults early in their lives from a number of significant sources. Your children are observant and absorbent beings, and as a result, they see and mimic the behavior of you, peers, and other people present in their lives. These early role models give children their first exposure to defaults. When your children see important people in their lives behaving in particular ways in different situations, they come to adopt those reactions as their own defaults. The power of this default-inducing effect is evident in simple ways, such as the body language and vocabulary your children pick up from you, to more complex ways, such as when your children produce emotional responses similar to your own in certain situations.

Ultimately, defaults are inculcated through consistent and repeated exposure. The messages your children see and hear the most will likely dictate how they act and react in similar situations. As your children develop their language capabilities, you can also influence their defaults through conversations about appropriate behavior and in discussions that arise during teachable moments. With sufficient repetition, these messages become ingrained as defaults that will have an enduring and resilient influence on future behavior.

Whether the defaults that your children establish are healthy or otherwise depends entirely on the quality of the messages they get from you and from the world they are immersed in. From this perspective, it's easy to see how the omnipresence of popular culture and technology can play a powerful role in the defaults that are established in your children.

Types of Defaults
Values

The values that your children internalize early in their lives become their first defaults and the gatekeepers that influence their particular course of action. When you send healthy value messages to your children—such as respect, honesty, and compassion—they, in turn, ingrain value defaults that are consistent with those value messages. Your children will be more likely to be respectful of others, to tell the truth, and to help others, respectively, when confronted with situations that trigger these value defaults.

The sad reality is that there are a whole lot of bad value messages that your children will be exposed to throughout their early years, mainly from popular culture, peers, and technology. Consequently, it becomes even more of a challenge to instill healthy values in your children.

As long as your children are in the protective cocoon of your home (i.e., before they head off to preschool and beyond), you have considerable control over those value messages. When, however, your children leave the safety of your nest, the preponderance of value messages will tilt heavily in the unhealthy direction. Your best hope, and your goal, is to communicate and instill positive value messages in your children while you have the greatest influence over them, thereby establishing value defaults early in their lives. With those healthy value defaults in place, your children will be more resistant to the unhealthy values they will be bombarded with as they enter school and the larger social and digital world.

Attitudes

The attitudes that your children hold about themselves, others, and their world—for example, self-esteem, delayed gratification, willingness to take risks, friendships, and hard work—will play a significant role in the path their lives take. Establishing healthy attitude defaults will help your children navigate the inevitable challenges, whether personal, academic, social, or professional, that they will face as they progress through life. These attitude defaults are initially instilled through your relationship with your children, the messages you send them about your attitude toward them, and the early experiences they have as they engage with their expanding world.

Physical Habits

As research shows, early physical habits related to diet, exercise, and sleep can set the stage for your children's long-term health (or ill health). These early habits become defaults that have very real implications for whether your children lead healthy and vigorous lives or sedentary lives filled with health and quality-of-life problems. Yet with incessant junk-food advertisements, for example, geared toward children, popular culture makes developing these positive defaults a real challenge. When you look at children's unhealthy dietary and exercise habits—coupled with the unhealthy defaults that are established at such a young age—you can understand why obesity among children has reached epidemic proportions and how that unhealthiness has profound negative ramifications throughout their lives. When you send messages about physical health to your children through leading an active life, preparing healthy meals and snacks, and encouraging them to be active, you take the first steps toward instilling healthy physical defaults that will serve them for a lifetime.

Free Time and Play

One of the most powerful ways in which early experiences influence your children's lives is how they learn to occupy their free time and play. For example, do they read or watch television in their free time? When they play, do they prefer to play tag outdoors or video games indoors? The defaults you establish in your children's early years for how they spend their free time and how they play will affect them for many years to come.

Early use (and overuse) of technology, including television, computers, and video games, is creating an entirely new set of defaults that were simply unavailable in generations past and that are now reshaping how children spend their free time and how they play.

How these new wired experiences will affect children in their ability to overcome boredom, be creative, and play with others is a matter of speculation at this point. At the same time, there is a growing body of research, which I discuss in part 2, that suggests the need for you as parents to be thoughtful and deliberate in your children's exposure to technology. Healthy free-time and play defaults will, ideally, encourage your children to take initiative; to be imaginative and inventive; and, importantly, to learn to overcome boredom and entertain themselves without undue reliance on popular culture and technology. Nevertheless, these defaults will also include varying degrees of technology, to be determined by your values and sensibilities.

Social Skills

Children establish their social comfort and skills early in their lives by observing you in your own social life and through the social experiences they have. These first social experiences become the defaults that will guide and shape the quality and quantity of their relationships throughout their lives. Genetics clearly has an influence on these defaults; research has demonstrated that children are born with a certain temperament, including where they lie on the continuum of introversion to extraversion. But, as the saying goes, "genetics are not destiny"; the messages that your children get from you early in their lives about how they should interact with others will influence how their genetic predispositions will be expressed. In this interaction of genes and upbringing, your children will develop social defaults that trigger social ease, connectedness, and healthy relationships, or social anxiety, loneliness, and dysfunctional relationships.

No Guarantees, But...

If you expose your children to all kinds of healthy messages early in their lives, does this guarantee that they will develop only positive defaults? Does it ensure that they won't do anything stupid, mean, or unhealthy in their lives? Of course not. All children are born with unique genetic compositions, such as temperament, that predispose them to certain defaults. For example, children who are born introverted will probably develop social defaults that lean toward shyness and social discomfort. Furthermore, even when your children are young, you aren't the only influence on them; they're exposed to other forces in their social world, such as their extended family, peers, or caregivers, who will have an effect on the defaults that they develop. And as human beings, there's just no way that you as parents can send your children only healthy messages; you will certainly convey some of your baggage and your own unhealthy defaults, and those, too, will have an impact on the social defaults that your children develop.

So, just as computers have bugs, glitches, lockups, and crashes, no matter how well they're programmed and maintained, your children will "malfunction" at times as well. They'll need to be refreshed and updated periodically. But, as long as your children are properly programmed (meaning that you've established healthy defaults in them) from the beginning, you can be confident that those darling little "computers" will function productively and happily for many years to come.

Parents Need Defaults Too

Defaults don't just apply to your children; they can also have a significant impact on your parenting. Think of it this way: when you become a parent, you send many different messages to your children, consciously and unconsciously. Through sheer repetition, the messages you communicate become defaults that determine the subsequent messages you convey to your children. If you unwittingly send unhealthy messages to your children early in their lives, those messages can become established in you as defaults. Your preset option in the future will be to continue to transmit those less-than-positive messages. The same holds true for positive messages that you initially communicate to your children. That's why it's as important for you as it is for your children to begin their lives with mindful and deliberate messages.

Your children aren't the only ones who are susceptible to unhealthy messages from popular culture, peers, and other forces in your community. You, too, have some of the same needs as your children, such as the needs to be liked, to be accepted, or to feel "normal." Just like your children, those needs can cause you to be swayed by outside forces with messages that are just as harmful to you as they are to your children. You may feel pressure from your peers to keep up with the Joneses, such as by being more concerned about your children's academic achievements than their personal development. Seeing what other parents are doing for their children, such as putting them in many extracurricular activities and camps, may push your buttons, causing you to internalize those messages, such as by pushing your children to do things that satisfy your needs but aren't best for them—and this will become your default.

Now you can begin to see the importance of establishing healthy defaults in your own parenting; the practice of sending positive messages to your children early and consistently causes you to ingrain the process of sending healthy messages, which, in turn, become your messaging defaults. As you and your children are increasingly exposed to the big, cruel world, you will have already established your own positive defaults that will help you resist toxic messages and will increase your children's chances of establishing healthy defaults.

Raising Kids 3.0: Setting Defaults

- Identify the ways in which technology can benefit your children.

- Identify the ways in which technology can hurt your children.

- List the defaults that your children have related to popular culture and technology.

- List the defaults that you have related to popular culture and technology.

- Identify the value, attitude, health, free-time and play, and social defaults that you would like your children to develop.

- Consider making changes on the basis of what you've learned about your and your children's defaults related to popular culture and technology.

Chapter 4
An Unmediated Life Worth Living

"I prefer, in short, a world cloaked in virtual intimacy. It may be electronic, but it is intimacy nevertheless. Besides, eye contact isn't all it's cracked up to be and facial expressions can be so hard to control. My life goes like this: every morning, before I brush my teeth, I sign in to my instant messenger to let everyone know I'm awake. I check for new email, messages or views, bulletins, invitations, friend requests, comments on my blog, or mentions of me or my blog on my friends' blogs."

—*Theodora, twentysomething blogger*

To this point, I've surveyed the current cultural and technological landscape you're raising your children in and, hopefully, have convinced you of the importance of establishing early and positive defaults in your children. Now, before we wade into part 2 of the book and explore how popular culture and technology are negatively and positively influencing your children, I want to provide you with a big-picture sense of the kind of life that I believe your children should lead during their formative years. This life should result in their developing into Kids 3.0: children who have both the old-school values, attitudes, and tools and the new-school technological skills that will enable them to thrive in the twenty-first century.

Unmediated Life

At the heart of this life I advocate for is your children's ability to live a largely unmediated life that offers them direct access to their experiences. In this book, the meaning of *unmediated* is twofold. First, so many children these days are forced to view their world through the lens of popular culture. Popular culture is present in everything they watch, read, and listen to; even the things they eat, wear, and play with can be tied to popular culture. It doesn't take a great stretch of the imagination to see how these popular culture lenses would have a significant impact on how your children come to view themselves and their world. You want your children to see themselves and their lives unencumbered by these lenses so that they can experience life in a pure and unbiased way, thus allowing them to decide for themselves on the meaning of popular culture and how it might affect them.

Second, as the research I discussed previously suggests, children spend an astonishing amount of their time in front of screens, whether televisions, computers, video-game consoles, or smartphones. As I will describe shortly, this mediated experience of life in front of screens has significant limitations for and real implications on their development. You want your children to experience most of their life directly, free from the very virtual representations of life rendered through a screen.

Three Dimensions of Life

Your children should experience their lives in three dimensions. New developments have allowed three-dimensional movies, video games, and other forms of technology to become available, but don't be fooled into thinking it's the same thing. For example, 3-D movies, video games, and smartphones provide the illusion of three dimensions, but, in reality, they continue to be two dimensional. Though they certainly add entertainment value, there is, nonetheless, no substitute for the true three-dimensionality of real life.

There is no research on this topic to date, but it seems reasonable to speculate that so much time devoted to the two-dimensional world of technology could hurt your children's processing of the three-dimensional world. As much as possible, you want your children to perceive and interact with all three dimensions of the world as it exists in reality, not with a virtual world missing a dimension.

Complete Sensory Experiences

Real life is also satisfying thanks to the rich sensory experience it provides: sight, sound, smell, touch, taste, balance, movement, temperature, pain, and emotions (not exactly a sense per se, but emotions are experienced acutely in sensory form). Yes, technology has made great advances in replicating real-life experiences: video games have improved visual graphics and sound, and Wiis and Xbox Kinects can replicate our movements and balance on a TV screen. Technology can even give us emotionally evocative content, although its typically artificially created and irrelevant to real life (e.g., FarmVille) or kept at arm's length (e.g., Facebook).

It seems likely that the substitution of a complete sensory experience with one that is lacking, fragmented, or mediated in its sensory output could have developmental ramifications for your children. You want your children to consume the depth and intensity of the full spectrum of sensory information that is available to them through unmediated living.

Open-Ended Experiences

Technology, by its very nature, puts children in a box, a very bright, shiny, and fun box to be sure, but a box nonetheless. This box is based on technology's necessity to restrict the options it programs into software. You may think those dropdown menus give your children options, but what they really do is limit their choices. When your children are placed in a box, they have no incentive or capability to think or act outside of that box, which is what creativity is all about.

Also, because technology provides a complete package (e.g., narrative, visuals) in TV shows, movies, and video games, little is left to children's imaginations; they become consumers of others' creativity rather than producers of their own. Imagination and creativity are muscles that will develop only if exercised.

Real life offers children experiences that are open ended, thus giving them the opportunity to flex those muscles. They're free to create whatever box they choose (or create no box at all) from the universe of options that are available in the real world. The only limits that exist are those set by children's imaginations and the physical parameters of real life (which rarely hold them back). Isn't it a true marvel to watch a child engage in imaginary play with nothing more than a few props? The worlds, characters, and story lines that children create are remarkable. You want your children to have that freedom to explore what is possible (and even impossible), and those opportunities cannot be found in the virtual world.

Values

Real life is value driven, which means that the direction in which children take their lives is based on what they value. As a result, life has personal meaning and relevance to them. With that meaning and relevance comes investment, that is to say, caring about what they do and where their lives lead them. Popular culture has little interest in values unless it involves instilling those values in children that will increase the bottom line.

Technology, in turn, is value neutral; how it is used determines its relationship with values. Susan Greenfield, a noted British neuroscientist who has studied the impact of new technology on children, has argued that for much of the technology your children will be immersed in, process, action, and achieving goals are the focal points, with little regard for personal values, meaning, or relevance.

Technology can be used with values in mind, for example, relationships, creativity, and social justice. Realistically, though, values aren't usually a significant force behind children's relationship with technology.

The connection between real life and values is perhaps the most powerful disincentive for an essential role of popular culture and technology in your children's lives. The bottom line is that most of popular culture and technology simply don't matter because they are devoid of values, meaning, and relevance; in other words, children's actions in those realms just don't have much of an impact on children's lives. Yes, they can offer fun and entertainment, but without values, meaning, and relevance, they are undeserving of a central place in children's lives.

In contrast, real life does matter, because children's actions directly affect their lives. This influence gives their lives the meaning and relevance that is lacking in popular culture and technology. As children mature and become aware of the role of values in their lives, they become the principal guides to how children think, feel, and behave.

Think of it this way: If your children no longer had popular culture in their lives, would anything beyond fun and entertainment be lost? If they no longer used technology for anything other than communication and educational purposes, would there be a gaping hole in their existences? In both cases, I would suggest not. Which would you rather have guiding your children's lives: the healthy values that you've instilled in them or the toxic values of popular culture or the absent values in technology?

Context

Real life has context, which means that it occurs within a framework of time (past, present, and future), relationships (your children and other people), and consequences (what your children do has an effect on the world). Yes, later in life popular culture and technology gain context because they exist within and are an extension of real life. But for children, much of the popular culture and technology that they are involved in lacks context, because when they use those things, time seems suspended from the normal timeline of their lives. Also, because much of children's involvement with popular culture and technology occurs either alone or through virtual connections, they lack the context of real relationships. What children do as they, for example, watch television or movies or play video games or surf the Internet, has no direct consequences on their lives or the lives of others. You want your children to spend most of their time in the context of real life because it is in that context that children are able to gain perspective on time, relationships, and consequences that are vital to their healthy development.

Physicality

Real life is physical, which means that much of what children do in their lives involves physical action and an understanding of the place that their physical being holds in the world they live in. Most of technology lacks or limits this essential physical component: children sit passively in front of a television or simulate actual physical activities with a Wii.

Yet, as developing physical beings, children need physicality to be a central part of their lives. Given the obesity epidemic among children today, regular physical activity has immense ramifications on children's and our nation's futures. Physical activity like sports and dance—not the simulated variety found with technology—is essential for the healthy development of motor skills.

A great challenge that all children face, particularly as they enter puberty, is to feel comfortable and confident in their bodies. This experience is especially difficult today with popular culture offering unrealistic and often unhealthy physical role models. Images of beautiful and thin women and handsome and muscular men are ubiquitous, and so-called physical imperfections can be easily corrected with cosmetic surgery.

Children should use physical activity to learn about and feel at ease with their bodies; without this activity, they're at risk of becoming victims of popular culture and technology, which does no favors for children in their physical lives.

Relationships

Finally, and perhaps most important, real life, and much of the meaning, satisfaction, and happiness accrued from it, comes from our relationships with others. The development of your children's social lives is essential for much of their future psychological and emotional well-being. In fact, considerable research has found that the quality of relationships is the single best predictor of happiness.

Yet using technology—like watching television or movies, playing video games alone, or surfing the Web—doesn't allow for the development of relationships. Yes, some technology, like Facebook, texting, and multiplayer video games, has a social component, but technology also has serious limitations. First, relationships that are based in technology seem to be "social lite," because children can't experience the real richness of human interactions (e.g., facial expressions, body language, emotional content). Second, they are "social safe," because such relationships are kept at a comfortable distance, thus protecting children from the risks and hurt (along with the benefits and joys) of real social interaction.

Don't get me wrong. There is certainly a place for technology in children's social lives. Facebook, Skype, and other technologies pro-vide many avenues to help children begin and maintain relationships. Interactive video or online games are certainly better than watching TV or movies with others, which are generally passive and asocial experiences for children. Are these social forms of technology as good as or better than playing tag, wiffle ball, or dress up? I'm going to vote no on that one. You want your children to be immersed in a predominantly rich and unmediated social life that offers everything they need to develop into socially comfortable, confident, and connected people.

High-Res Life

I'm going to once again borrow a term from the tech world that has tremendous relevance to your children's world. That word is *resolution*, which refers to the clarity and sharpness of an image, whether a printed photograph or an image viewed on a computer screen (usually defined in terms of pixels or dots per inch). Now, you might be wondering what resolution has to do with your children. Here's how: technology cre-ates a low-resolution approximation of reality that offers an incomplete experience lacking granularity, or richness, complexity, and—as I previ-ously noted—three dimensionality. Yes, it offers practical benefits and entertainment value, but is it high resolution enough to substitute for your children's real lives? I don't believe so.

When I refer to high resolution, I mean the full sensory experience of real life, but I also mean its entire social and emotional experience. Life is often risky, messy, difficult, and sometimes hurtful. But life is two sides of the same coin. Your children can't experience the meaning, satisfaction, and joy of life unless you allow them to also experience its less pleasant sides. You want your children to experience a high-resolution life that is unmediated, unfiltered, and unlimited (with your guidance, of course).

Only with such high-resolution experiences will your children develop the capabilities to prosper in the real world they live in; technology should make up only a small part of their world.

Certainly, technology can play a role in your children's real lives; it can be a source of entertainment, and children will need to learn how to use it to lead productive lives. However, I think you would agree that it shouldn't be a free, unfettered, and dominant force in your children's lives. If that happens, your children will miss out on so much good stuff that makes unmediated life far better and more interesting than a mediated life could possibly offer.

What Life Do You Choose for Your Children?

There is, as they say, more than one road to Rome. I can't offer you a clear and well-defined path that you should take in raising your children in this world so dominated by popular culture and technology. Everything I write about in this book addresses issues that are not black and white but rather many shades of gray. Which shade of gray you choose depends on your own values and attitudes, your relationship with technology, your understanding of how popular culture and technology influence your children, and the goals that you have for them.

The real point of *Raising Generation Tech* is to convey the importance of being well informed and deliberate in how you expose your children to popular culture and technology. You can use these criteria of a balanced childhood that includes both unmediated and mediated experiences to evaluate your children's relationship with popular culture and technology and to determine how you can guide them toward having a balanced childhood themselves.

Raising Kids 3.0: Unmediated Life

- Keep track of and compare how much mediated and unmediated experience your children have outside of school.

- What aspects of unmediated life are your children missing in their involvement with popular culture and technology?

- What types of unmediated experience would you like your children to have more of?

- Make a list of ways in which you can reduce the amount of mediated experience and increase the amount of unmediated experience your children have.

Part II

Protect and Prepare Your Children

Chapter 5

Self-Identity: Who Are They?

"To all of Chris' friends: This is his father. My son carelessly left his account logged in so I decided to snoop around. Upon reading my son's personal information, I would like to clear a few things up. My son is not a 'gangsta,' he will not 'beat a ho's ass,' and he will most certainly not 'roll a fatty wit his boyz.' So for all of those who think he is some hard ass thug, think again...he is Chris _____, a 15-year-old kid that was afraid of the dark until he was 12 and cried at the end of Marley and Me.*"*

—*Father who changed his son's Facebook status*

Is there anything more important to your children's long-term development than the formation of a healthy self-identity? Self-identity encompasses the totality of the knowledge and understanding that children gain about themselves, including their personalities, aptitudes and capabilities, intellectual and physical attributes, interests, and relationships. Self-identity includes not only present perceptions but also future and idealized self-conceptions that act as the aspirations and goals that children strive toward. How your children come to think of themselves, define who they are as people, and see themselves as unique all play a vital role in the people they become and the direction their lives take.

Self-identity also involves two separate, though related, mechanisms: self-awareness and self-esteem. Self-awareness refers to your children's ability to be introspective and understand who they are, such as understanding their personality, values, needs, attitudes, and emotions. Self-esteem is your children's general evaluation of their competence and worth as a person based on what they know of themselves from their self-awareness and self-concept.

As children mature, their self-identities become clearly defined. Healthy self-identity is internally and externally congruent, which means that the perceptions that children hold about themselves are consistent with one another. Also, because feedback from the world they live in helps form children's self-identities, those perceptions are not in conflict with that external feedback.

Importantly, a healthy self-identity provides children with three essential senses that act as the foundation for future development. First, self-identity gives children a sense of consistency and stability over time, thus helping them to feel safe, secure, and comfortable in exploring the limits of their abilities. Second, it gives children a sense of uniqueness, which allows them to seek out their own individual place and make special contributions to the world. Third, self-identity gives them a sense of affiliation: while they see themselves as distinct beings, they also feel like an integral part of a group and capable of building nurturing relationships in different aspects of their lives.

Externalization of Self-Identity

One aspect of self-identity that is particularly relevant to Kids 3.0 is that children gain their self-identity through self-observation and information from their social world. As children gain self-awareness, they observe and evaluate their own behavior on the basis of past experience, current needs, and future goals and dreams. They also look outward to the world they live in, for example, social, academic, and physical, for feedback that shapes their self-identity. Because children are fundamentally social beings, and an essential part of their development involves finding their place in the social and cultural context they live in, feedback from that social world plays a significant role in the evolution of their self-identity.

Because children's social worlds have expanded dramatically in the past decade, from families, friends, neighborhoods, and schools to an almost-limitless universe of people given the proliferation of the Internet, it isn't difficult to see how external forces may be gaining a disproportionate influence over the development of children's self-identity compared to previous generations, for whom social worlds were far more confined. These social influences, accelerated by the explosion of technology, may be interfering with healthy development of self-identity in children.

One of the most powerful ways that popular culture and technology are altering the way in which self-identities are established in children is through the shift from being internally to externally driven. Yes, as I just described, social factors have always had an impact on the formation of self-identity, but, until recently, they had been equal partners of sorts with children's own internal contributors to self-identity. Now the sheer ubiquity and force of recent technological advances has tipped the scale of that influence heavily in the direction of external forces.

In previous generations, most of the social forces that influenced children's self-identities were positive; parents, peers, schools, communities, people involved in their extracurricular activities, and even the media sent mostly healthy messages to children about who they were and how they should perceive themselves. Yes, there were bad influences, but beneficial influences far outweighed the bad. These forces acted mostly as a mirror reflecting back on children what they saw in themselves, resulting in affirmation rather than change in their self-identities.

But now the pendulum has swung to the other extreme: a social world in which the profit motive trumps concern for children's well-being and in which the cacophony of popular culture as transmitted by the latest technology mostly drowns out healthy influences.

The self-identities of this generation of children are now molded by external forces in two ways. First, popular culture, through the media of today's technology, no longer holds up a mirror to reflect children's self-identities. Nor does it provide feedback about how grounded their self-identities are in the reality of their lives. Instead, popular culture manipulates self-identities to serve its selfish interests, thus causing children to, for example, excessively identify themselves by their physical appearance or the material goods they own. Tapping into children's most basic needs to feel good about themselves, accepted, and attractive, popular culture tells children what they should believe about themselves. The problem is that the self-identity that popular culture shapes serves its own best interests rather than those of children. In addition, self-identity is no longer really derived from the self; rather, it is an identity projected onto children by popular culture, and it is in no way a reflection of who children are, what the British neuroscientist Susan Greenfield calls the nobody scenario.

Second, technology has caused children to shift away from expressing their self-identities and toward constructing a facade based on the answers to two questions: How will others look at me? and How can I ensure that others view me positively? Children's goal in their use of technology, whether it be Facebook, YouTube, Twitter, or text messaging, becomes how they can curry acceptance, popularity, status, and—by extension—self-esteem. For example, research indicates that young people are beginning to base their self-esteem on the number of "friends" they accumulate on Facebook. Healthy self-awareness and self-expression give way to an unhealthy preoccupation with what others think, impression management, and self-promotion. As the writer Christine Rosen wrote in her

2007 article in the *New Atlantis*, "Does this technology, with its constant demands to collect (friends and status), and perform (by marketing ourselves), in some ways undermine our ability to attain what it promises—a surer sense of who we are and where we belong? The Delphic oracle's guidance was *know thyself*. Today, in the world of online social networks, the oracle's advice might be *show thyself*."

Children come to see their identities not as expressions of who they are and what they believe, but rather the identities they would like to have or that they want people to see. They then feel compelled to promote and market those identities using technology rather than embracing and expressing internally generated and accurate expressions of who they really are and who they really want to be.

The line between person and persona, private and public self, becomes blurred or erased completely, and the so-called self-identity, which is supposed to be a reflection of the individuality of each child, becomes a means of being validated by others in their digital communities. Yet when children manipulate their personas in their extensive efforts to be, for example, "liked" on Facebook, they come to believe that they're not worthy of being liked (in the original sense of the word) for who they really are.

Paradoxically, in striving for approval from their social world writ large through technology, and in seeking uniqueness that enables children to stand out in the densely populated cyberworld, they unwittingly sacrifice their true self-identities and shape their identities to conform to what the digital world views as acceptable. In doing so, children relinquish the specialness that they hold so dear. Notes Christine Rosen, "Indeed, this is one of the characteristics of MySpace [her article was written before Facebook surpassed MySpace] most striking to anyone who spends a few hours trolling its millions of pages: it is an overwhelmingly dull sea of monotonous uniqueness, of conventional individuality, of distinctive sameness." Because children's needs for acceptance and status are so strong, and the external forces so powerful and pervasive, they have little choice but to capitulate and adopt the identities that are imposed on them rather than seeking out their true self-identities.

Primed Children

Media priming is a psychological concept that explains the power of popular culture to create an externalized identity in children. Media priming "refers to the residual, often unintended consequences of media use on subsequent perceptions, judgments, and behavior." In other words, the messages popular culture sends through media stimulate related thoughts. For example, playing violent video games primes children to think, make judgments, and behave in ways that are consistent with those violent messages. Similar priming can be triggered by popular culture about sexuality, wealth, materialism, physical appearance, and other commonly communicated messages.

As an example, one study reported that frequent consumption of male-oriented media (movies, television, music videos, and men's magazines) significantly influenced young men's attitudes toward abstinence (less likely to abstain from sex), the male sexual role (more traditional views of women), casual sex (more acceptable), and their sexual behavior (more partners). Research has also shown that repetition and related associations of a message make the priming effect even more powerful and enduring.

With the 24/7 nature of technology today, it is easy to see how children, who, as I noted earlier, lack well-developed executive functioning capabilities, such as critical thinking, would be easy prey for the relentless priming messages that popular culture conveys.

The good news in this otherwise bad-news story is that there is a way to mitigate and even reverse media priming. Research has shown that children who are informed about the effects of these media messages or are offered a contrasting perspective to those messages are less likely to assimilate the messages and more resistant to their priming effects. For example, parents who talked to their children about the unhealthy effects of playing violent video games and established that violent behavior is unacceptable are more resistant to those messages that encourage violence.

Creation of a False Self

The externalization of self-identity may result in your children creating a false self, in which they internalize the messages of popular culture, such as valuing themselves on the basis of their appearance or popularity, and those messages become their self-identity. These unrelenting messages that children receive from popular culture through its many technological conduits and the development of the false self enable them to meet the demands of the manufactured world they're immersed in. Yet the cost is high: children create a false self that is incongruent with their true self, or their self-identity that is an expression of who they really are and the otherwise healthy world they live in.

The false self is constructed to satisfy the needs of popular culture, in particular, to generate more profit for those companies that control popular culture. Popular culture's emphasis on those needs, for example, to feel attractive and popular, results in children feeling psychologically, emotionally, and socially undernourished because these aspects of the false self don't satisfy their most basic needs for love, security, competence, and connection. In the absence of real meaning and fulfillment in their lives, children become dependent on popular culture and technology to meet the immediate and superficial needs of the externally constructed false self that provides them with only the bare minimum of nourishment to survive.

Children who are allowed to immerse themselves excessively in popular culture and use technology freely and frequently are faced with a choice that really isn't a choice. They can remain true to their emerging self-identity and forsake what they perceive as acceptance and validation by much of their social world (which is controlled by popular culture and technology), or they can accept the false self that has been contrived by popular culture and ensure its ongoing esteem, however unhealthy, at the price of losing their real self-identity. As children's exposure to popular culture and technology grows, so does the pressure to repress their burgeoning true self, with its positive perspectives and healthy needs, and allow their false self, with its faulty judgments and dangerous prohibitions, to gain dominance.

Here is a wake-up call for you: if your own messages are reinforcing popular culture's messages, your children have little chance but to capitulate to the externalized identity that is being forced on them. Imagine the two most powerful forces in their lives, popular culture and you, sending them the same messages to forsake their internally emerging self-identity for one that is in direct conflict with it. The need to gain love and approval from you *and* to be accepted and valued by popular culture gives them no other option than to bury their true self-identity deep inside and allow the false self to come to the fore and assert control.

On their own, it's virtually impossible for your children to resist the external identity and false self that popular culture communicates through its many forms of influence. For example, children may feel compelled by the need to be accepted to value what their peers value (and, by the way, peers are the minions of popular culture), such as an emphasis on physical appearance or being cruel to members of an out-group at school, even if those values are in conflict with those of their family and themselves. Your children lack the experience, perspective, and maturity to withstand the pressure, particularly when coming from their immediate social world.

Self-Esteem

Overexposure to popular culture and excessive dependence on technology can cause children to value themselves on the basis of the messages they get from the former and the feedback they receive from the latter. There is a robust body of research that affirms this statement. For example, girls who read fashion and celebrity magazines, compared to those who don't, are more self-conscious about their bodies, diet and exercise more, and are more vulnerable to eating disorders. Also, the sexualization of females that dominates both old and new media and is accessible to increasingly younger girls results in distorted body images, low self-esteem, and depression, among other developmental problems. Among boys, research has shown that unrealistic portrayals of men related to physical prowess, appearance, intellect, and attractiveness to the opposite sex create unrealistic expectations that lower self-esteem.

New technology, such as the Internet, Facebook, and text messages, is playing a growing role in the formation and maintenance of self-esteem in children. There is growing evidence that young people are increasingly basing how they feel about themselves on how connected they are and the quantity of their relationships. The steady influx of text messages, regular postings on social networking sites, and number of "likes" and "friends" they have, for example, become the measures of children's self-worth. The absence of those things becomes the grounds for doubt, insecurity, and anxiety.

There is an emerging body of evidence indicating that children's self-esteem is developing an unhealthy relationship with social media. For example, one study found that Facebook users who had low self-esteem posted more "self-promotional" materials (e.g., complimentary photos and status messages) on their pages than those with high self-esteem. Another study reported that participants whose self-esteem was affected more by outside influences were more likely to spend more time and post more photos of themselves on Facebook.

So far, I've painted a pretty bleak picture of technology's impact on children's self-esteem. There is, however, evidence of its value in the development of children's self-esteem. For example, one study found that social media provides opportunities to build self-esteem, develop friendships, and hone social skills. Other research reported that Facebook users experienced boosted self-esteem when they viewed or edited their profiles or received feedback from friends, not surprising given that both tend to be positive. In addition, the sense of security that social media provides can allow shy children to express themselves more and practice social skills, which can then translate into more confidence and comfort in social interactions and, as a result, greater self-esteem.

Consistent with my message throughout *Raising Generation Tech*, popular culture and technology will be harmful to children's self-esteem only if they are exposed to them in excess, without reasonable filters, guidance, perspective, or sufficient counterbalances, such as positive experiences, feedback, or messages in the real world.

Narcissism on the Rise

Ironically, the externalization of self-identity has resulted in an unhealthy internal focus on the self. Do you recall the story of Narcissus? After he displayed indifference and disdain toward others, the gods punished this handsome fellow in Greek mythology by forcing him to fall in love with his own image. He was so enrapt by his own beauty that he was unable to pull himself away from his reflection in a pool of water and wasted away and died.

Just so we are all on the same wavelength, narcissism is a personality characteristic associated with self-absorption, egocentrism, an overestimation of one's own importance and abilities, a sense of entitlement, and a disregard for others. Narcissus seems to have spawned many offspring in our current generation; according to research, narcissism is alive and well in America. Using a widely used psychological test, one recent study found that 30 percent of young people were classified as narcissistic (that number has doubled in the past thirty years). Another study reported a 40 percent decline among young people in empathy, a personality attribute inversely related to narcissism, since the 1980s. These findings aren't surprising to anyone who pays attention to the "it's all about me" culture in which we currently live. So what has caused this rise in narcissism, and what impact will it have on our children?

Young people are learning about narcissism from popular culture. A study by the celebrity psychiatrist Dr. Drew Pinsky, in which two hundred "celebrities" (I put the word in quotes because the bar for being considered a celebrity is set very low these days) completed the Narcissistic Personality Inventory, found that they were significantly more narcissistic than the general population. Interestingly, the celebrities who actually had a talent, such as musicians, tended to be less narcissistic. Who were the most self-absorbed celebrities? Female reality-TV stars! It is not surprising that celebrities who were famous for being famous were the most narcissistic; their narcissism drove them to become celebrities.

Another fascinating study explored the changes in music lyrics over the past three decades. Researchers found a significant shift toward lyrics that reflect narcissism (*I* and *me* appear more often than *we* and *us*) and hostility (angry words and emotions appear more often than positive terms). These findings aren't just a result of the increased popularity and influence of hip-hop music (which is known for its aggrandizement of the artists and its venom); they're evident across musical genres. You don't need to go far to collect your own data on narcissism. Do Charlie Sheen, Terrell Owens, or Kanye West ring a bell?

It's not surprising to see a rise in narcissism in this generation, given that young people are being bombarded by these messages through every form of media, including social networking sites and celebrity Twitter feeds. Many commentators have called websites such as Facebook and Twitter receptacles of narcissism, because they give children outlets for sharing the trivial and for gaining attention. In addition, the time spent immersed in technology has likely done its part to promote narcissism. All the time spent in front of screens has reduced the amount of face-to-face contact that children have, thus depriving them of the experiences needed to develop essential social skills that counter narcissism, such as empathy, compassion, and consideration for others.

Here's the truly disturbing part: how can children these days avoid being infected with this "disease" when, thanks to the wired world they live in, the majority of messages they receive venerate and encourage narcissism?

The self-esteem movement and the recent shift toward hyperparent-ing has also likely contributed to this increase in self-adoration. Although the specific causes of narcissism have not been confirmed, researchers have identified a number of factors that increase the likelihood that a child will become narcissistic: (1) being praised for innate qualities such as physical appearance, intelligence, or other abilities; (2) receiving praise that is inconsistent with reality; (3) earning extreme rewards for good behavior and undue criticism or punishment for bad behavior; (4) being spoiled and excessively indulged by parents; and (5) having parents whose self-esteem is overly invested in their children's achievements. Moreover, children who are born with a sensitive temperament are more vulnerable to these parenting approaches.

In addition to the unsettling rise in narcissism among our children, perhaps a greater concern is that our culture seems to not only accept but also promote narcissism as the norm. The shift in societal values away from collectivism and toward individualism, away from civic responsibility and toward self-gratification, and away from meaningful contributions to society and toward personal success (as defined by wealth, power, celebrity, and status) have also contributed to the cultural messages of narcissism in which children are presently immersed.

There is no doubt that narcissists in popular culture are worshipped (narcissism is cool), and new technology is used to a great extent to feed that narcissism to the masses (what else could explain why Ashton Kutcher has more than seven million Twitter followers?). Additionally, the indifference, egotism, disrespect, and lack of consideration that are central to narcissism also reflect the increasingly polarized and vitriolic tone of our current body politic, recent unethical corporate behavior, the rise in cheating among students in school, and the gamut of bad behavior among professional athletes. Children who are exposed to a culture that sends messages that "it's all about me" will likely fall prey to those messages.

That's when we have to start asking the next question, which is far scarier: what effect will this narcissistic culture have on our children and the development of their self-identities? Think of all the qualities that enable your children to become healthy and contributing members of our society (e.g., hard work, respect, compassion, tolerance, selflessness), and you will find that they don't exist in the narcissistic personality or the culture in which it is fostered.

Self-Identity in Kids 3.0

Self-identity is one of the trickier contributors to children's healthy development, because, as parents, you can't do things to your children to give them their self-identity. Rather, you can only create an environment that allows their self-identity to evolve naturally. Nevertheless, protecting your children from forces that aim to stunt, distort, or co-opt their self-identities can help support the emergence of healthy self-identities.

Of course, the obvious recommendation is to monitor and restrict your children's use of technology, from old-school media such as television and magazines to new-school media such as texting and social networking sites, so your children's exposure to the forces that cause an externalization of their self-identity is prevented, or at least minimized. But, let's be realistic, as digital natives, your children are going to be immersed in the tech world, so such a defensive posture probably will not be adequate in safeguarding your children against its ill effects.

Based on the latest research, here are some recommendations on how to help your children develop healthy self-identities amid the cacophony of messages they're getting from popular culture and the latest technology.

Emphasize Healthy Values

As I discuss in detail in chapter 6, you should focus on healthy values that help shape your children's self-identities, for example, integrity, hard work, respect, responsibility, and compassion. Being a role model of healthy values, talking about values, surrounding your children with value-driven people, and giving your children experiences that reinforce values are just a few of the ways that you can shape your children's values and protect them from the corrosive values of popular culture. When you emphasize values, you're also sending the message that the values your children will be exposed to through popular culture and technology aren't important to you.

Inoculate Your Children against Popular Culture's Messages

The research on media priming that I discussed earlier suggests that you can help your children resist popular culture's messages by priming them against it. When you consistently offer your children perspectives different from the negative messages they receive from popular culture, you prime them to stand firm against the unhealthy messages. You can help your children become sensitive to popular culture's messages by sharing their popular culture activities with them and pointing out and discussing the unhealthy messages that you observe. This will enable them to learn to recognize those messages for what they are and view them with a healthy skepticism. You can also actively teach your children executive functioning skills, such as critical thinking and long-term planning, by, for example, guiding them through a deliberate process of decision making, from identifying the options to making the final decision, which will further gird them against those messages.

Highlight Your Children's Intrinsic Passions and Strengths

Popular culture and technology are telling your children that they should value themselves on the basis of, for example, what they look like or what they have. You should be telling them that they should value themselves on the basis of their unique capabilities, such as their academic, athletic, or artistic achievements; their relationships with family and friends; their passions and interests; and anything else they believe, feel, or do that originates inside of themselves.

Keep Your Children Grounded in Reality

Popular culture and technology bombard your children with messages that are out of touch with reality. With persistent exposure, as the concept of media priming explains, these unrealistic messages and images can become your children's reality and, by extension, will negatively affect their self-identities. Your goal is to constantly expose your children to the real world, namely the one that is grounded in positive values, accurate depictions of appropriate behavior, reasonable expectations and consequences, and the inevitable imperfections and failures that are part of the human condition.

Have Your Children Involved in Healthy Activities

The best way to keep your children away from unhealthy influences is to keep them busy with healthy activities. Help them find activities that they love doing and that promote a healthy self-identity, whether academic, sports, or the arts. Research has shown that, for example, girls and boys who play sports have higher self-esteem, get better grades, and have fewer drug problems and lower rates of sexual activity.

Create a Healthy Family Lifestyle

Your children will base much of their self-identities on their most immediate environment. If your family life is informed by healthy values, choices, activities, and relationships, your children are more likely to internalize those messages as their own. For example, you can consciously limit your family's involvement with popular culture and technology and share positive family experiences such as frequent dinners together, outdoor activities, and spiritual pursuits.

Surround Your Children with Healthy People

You can use the priming effect to your advantage by surrounding your children with healthy people who support everything that goes into the development of a positive self-identity. These healthy messages will not only prime your children to think, feel, and behave in beneficial ways;

they will also provide consistent exposure to contrasting healthy perspectives that can mitigate popular culture's priming effect and influences.

Talk and Listen to Your Children

Your children have a tremendous capacity to communicate with you about what is happening in their lives, both good and not so good. Unfortunately, they're often speaking in a language that parents don't understand. If you listen to their messages, verbal, emotional, and behavioral, you'll be better able to hear what they're trying to tell you, particularly when they're asking for help. For example, your children may complain about not liking school, but what they may be really saying is that they don't like the messages their peers are sending them. Also, don't be afraid to talk to your children, especially about topics that make you uncomfortable or that they may not want to hear, such as the previously mentioned messages from their peers. Although they may not always seem like they're listening, your children want your guidance and support because they know that they can't go it alone and they need you on their side.

Help Others

The one form of externalization of self-identity that is healthy is when your children direct their focus and energies away from themselves and onto helping others. Healthy self-identity is built when your children are not preoccupied with themselves and experience the intrinsic rewards of improving the lives of others. Experiences of giving to others can also counteract the narcissistic messages they may get from popular culture. I encourage you to make compassion and community service family values and experiences to be shared.

Walk the Walk on a Healthy Self-Identity

For much of your children's early lives, you are their most important influence. They initially look to you to decide who they should be, what they
should value, and what they should do. "Do as I say, not as I do" just doesn't
cut it when it comes to parenting. You need to make sure that you're living
the healthy life that you want them to lead. Whether it's the people you
interact with, the activities you're involved in, what you talk about, or
what you eat or drink, your self-identity, as expressed through how you
live your life, will dictate to a large extent your children's self-identity.

If you fall prey to popular culture's messages and develop a manufactured identity, your children have little chance of developing their own
self-identities. Be sure that you have your own internally derived and
well-defined self-identity and that they see it clearly. If they do, they will
follow your lead and seek to establish their own self-identities.

Raising Kids 3.0: Self-Identity

- Keep track of and compare how much mediated and
  unmediated experience your children have outside
  of school.

- What aspects of unmediated life are your children
  missing in their involvement with popular culture and
  technology?

- What types of unmediated experience would you like
  your children to have more of?

- Make a list of ways you can reduce the amount of mediated experience and increase the amount of unmediated experience your children have.

Chapter 6

Values: What Do Your Children Believe?

"I love [Henry David Thoreau's] message of living simply, authentically, and, perhaps above all, living deliberately—making choices consciously about the way you're going to live your life, not having life live you."

—*Susan, mother of three*

Values have gotten a bad rap. When most people think of values these days, they think of hot-button topics and the divisive battle between so-called red-state and blue-state values. They think of politicians, media talking heads, and other groups that use values to push their own agendas. As America's discussion of values has focused on these divisions, many parents have lost sight of the truly essential role that values play in their children's development. This misdirection has caused many parents to allow other forces, namely popular culture and technology, to direct and shape the values that their children adopt. Even worse, the very same forces have exerted an undue influence over many parents' own values, and as a result, they have become unwitting accomplices to the often-unhealthy influences of popular culture and technology.

It's not my place to tell you what you should value. I will nonetheless tell you that you should know what you value and make sure that your values are healthy for your family. Also, you should communicate those values clearly and consistently to your children. Convey values to your children as soon as they develop the ability to talk, listen, and understand consequences. You want to introduce them to what values are, their importance to your family, and the role they play in their lives as early as possible so that they develop positive values before they're fully immersed in the crazy new world of popular culture and technology that communicates mostly unhealthy values.

Why Are Values Important?

Values are one of the most important and influential contributors to your children's development. Let's consider what values are. At their most basic level, values are the beliefs that you hold most dearly about what is important to you. The values that your children accept as their own will establish their priorities, guide their decisions, and shape their behavior. Perhaps more than anything else, values act as a road map in determining the direction your children's lives take, dictating who they spend time with, the activities they participate in, and the career path that they choose. Quite simply, values will determine the people your children will become.

Think about the kinds of people you want your children to develop into. Now think about the values that they will need to adopt to become those kinds of people. Would honest, respectful, and responsible be on your list? How about committed and hardworking? Compassionate and tolerant? Here's a good exercise for you: make a list of all the values that you want your children to adopt. Next, ask yourself what values you're actively teaching them. Then, look at the world of popular culture and technology they're immersed in and carefully examine what values they're getting from those forces.

Like many children growing up in this crazy new world, your children may be exposed to and learning values that are less than admirable. If so, then you may need to step back, reevaluate the role that popular culture and technology play in their lives, and perhaps make some changes in your family life so that your children receive the value messages that you want them to get.

What Are Healthy Values?

As I previously noted, there is much disagreement over what constitutes healthy values. However, if we look beyond those divisive values that inspire such ill will, we will find many more values we all can agree on, regardless of our religious, political, or cultural beliefs. These healthy values, such as respect, responsibility, justice, compassion, tolerance, happiness, and many others, foster positive self-regard, moral behavior, meaningful relationships, consideration of others, and many other wonderful attributes in children.

What Are Unhealthy Values?

A useful way to teach your children healthy values is to identify unhealthy values and help them see the differences. Using examples such as greed, selfishness, and dishonesty can help you illustrate how these values harm your children, your family, your community, and our society as a whole. When your children express unhealthy values, show them how the values hurt them and your family. You can also point out examples of bad values in their social world as object lessons of how not to behave.

Popular Culture and Values

Through its many technological conduits, popular culture affects children's most basic level—the values that shape their lives. It promotes some of the worst values and disguises them as entertainment, and it can overwhelm your children with unhealthy value messages through their seeming 24/7 connection with technology. You probably don't notice half of the unhealthy messages being conveyed to your children because popular culture hides its value messages behind entertaining characters, engaging narratives, and fun music.

Reality TV, for example, has made the seven deadly sins—pride, avarice, envy, wrath, lust, gluttony, and sloth—attributes to be admired. Throw in selfishness, deceit, spite, humiliation, cruelty, and vengeance—all qualities seen and seemingly revered in popular culture—and you have the personification of the worst kind of person. Here's a scary statistic: the most popular show among teens is *Jersey Shore*, that repository of stupidity, superficiality, drunkenness, promiscuity, and wealth and celebrity without talent or effort.

Popular culture relies on two primary avenues for communicating its value messages and influencing your children. The first type of message is what I call a loudspeaker message, which is deafening, constant, and ever present. The shrillness of these messages is heard, seen, tasted, and felt, and they cannot be readily avoided. Examples of these loudspeaker messages are most kinds of popular culture, including movies (e.g., *Knocked Up*), video games (e.g., *Grand Theft Auto*), television (e.g., *The Bachelor*), and music (e.g., "Shoot 'Em Up," by Nas), in addition to less obvious loudspeaker messages from billboards and magazine ads.

The second type of message that popular culture uses to seduce your children is what I call a stealth message. These messages are usually hidden behind the entertaining characters, images, words, and music I just alluded to. All these conduits subtly tap into children's unconscious needs and wishes. Messages that create positive emotional reactions, such as commercials depicting an actress dancing while drinking Pepsi, or a basketball player winning a game while wearing a pair of Nikes, resonate on a deep level with children, causing them to want to feel that way too. Other stealth messages that tap into children's most basic needs, fears, and insecurities related to self-esteem, social acceptance, and physical attractiveness are particularly effective in manipulating children.

Just Plain Bad Values

How powerful are the value messages that popular culture is sending our children? According to a large body of research, the answer is very potent and pervasive. Although I'm obviously making a judgment on what good and bad values are, I think many parents would agree with my list of unhealthy values for children. The research demonstrates that bad values actually hurt your children. There are many values that you want to protect your children from adopting, but I'm going to focus on the three that I believe are most influenced by popular culture and new technology, most harmful to children's development, and that have research to support my stance. Don't let my short list prevent you from identifying the unhealthy values hurting your children and from taking steps to prevent your children from being exposed to those values.

Success at Any Cost

An unsettling aspect of popular culture's perspective on success is its imperative that success must be achieved at any cost. This culture of success causes children to believe that they must succeed in our culturally defined ways to be esteemed by society, peers, and—most sadly—their parents. Not surprisingly, this message has created a desperate need for success in children. When that need is combined with growing up in a culture filled with greed and fraud yet lacking culpability, children learn that they can use any and all means to attain that success.

This culture of avarice not only tolerates but also encourages this "win at all costs" mentality by modeling and messaging dishonesty, cheating, manipulation, and backstabbing. Examples of this distorted view of success abound in popular culture. Reality TV shows like *Survivor* relish lying and deception. Sports has seen the proliferation of illegal performance-enhancing drugs among star athletes, such as Barry Bonds, who are revered by young athletes.

This "the ends justify the means" attitude is starkly evident among high school students. Two recent surveys found that 75 percent of students had cheated on a test in the previous twelve months, as compared to only 25 percent in 1963 and 50 percent in 1993. Particularly unsettling is the finding that about 50 percent of high school students see nothing wrong with cheating.

The rationales that students use to justify their cheating are disturbing. One student commented, "I actually think cheating is good. A person who has an entirely honest life can't succeed these days." Another said, "We students know that the fact is we are almost completely judged on our grades. They are so important that we will sacrifice our own integrity to make a good impression." Finally, from a third student: "I believe cheating is not wrong. People expect us to attend seven classes a day, keep a 4.0 GPA, not go crazy, and turn in all of our work the next day. What are we supposed to do, fail?"

Technology now enables young people to cheat more creatively, with less effort, and with less chance of getting caught. For example, students can plagiarize written assignments with ease from the wealth of information on any subject they can find on the Internet. There are also websites from which students can purchase papers rather than actually write them.

Research has also found a social-contagion effect, which indicates that young people are more likely to cheat when those around them cheat.

When children hear or see others cheat, they assume that it's acceptable to cheat, or they feel that they must cheat to keep up with their peers. But before recent technological advancements, children were exposed to a small circle of contagions, such as a group of friends or a sports team. The Internet now exposes children to a much wider and more diverse range of contagions, from peers to professional athletes to politicians to businesspeople. Children can readily read news stories about cheating and see posts on Facebook in which peers brag about cheating. The messages from these contagions tell children that everyone cheats, it's OK to cheat, and they must cheat if they are going to keep up with those who are already cheating.

Disturbingly, cheating in high school and college doesn't appear to be something that young people grow out of. To the contrary, recent research indicates that those who cheat early in life are more likely to cheat later in life, for example, by lying to customers, bosses, or significant others, or by overstating insurance claims or falsifying tax returns.

This "just win, baby" message that children get from popular culture can also be life threatening. The use of illegal performance-enhancing drugs is present at all levels of athletics and is increasing among young athletes. Recent research indicates that between 4 percent and 12 percent of high school male athletes—five hundred thousand to one million by some estimates—said they had taken steroids. Pressure to make varsity teams, receive college scholarships, and pursue professional or Olympic success (however much of a pipe dream that is for all but a few) compels many young athletes to take drastic steps to improve performance. These athletes are heavily influenced by the professional athletes who are their role models. They see that the benefits of steroid use are significant and that the consequences of being caught are minimal. Barry Bonds, for example, saw his hitting production increase dramatically while taking performance-enhancing drugs, and he was rewarded with contracts worth hundreds of millions of dollars. Even when he was convicted of lying about his drug use to a grand jury during a federal investigation, his sentence was a mere slap on the wrist.

The invincibility that many teenagers feel precludes them from considering the health risks of steroid use, which include infertility, high blood pressure, liver damage, and prostate cancer. Young athletes also ignore the psychological and emotional dangers of steroid use, for example, hyperaggression (what is known as 'roid rage), irritability, and, upon their discontinuation, depression, lethargy, and feelings of hopelessness. A study attributed at least two suicides to steroid withdrawals in recent years, as well as an undetermined number of suicide attempts.

This unprincipled attitude toward success is one of the most powerful indications of popular culture's and technology's corruption of children in America. This is the crazy new world in which your children are growing up. With so much of popular culture sending messages to your children through its technological conduits that it's OK to lie, cheat, steal, be irresponsible, and act selfishly, how can your children not come to the conclusion that such behavior is not only perfectly acceptable but also absolutely necessary to find success in life?

Wealth and Materialism

Money certainly has great value. Money provides for basic needs, such as food, clothing, and shelter, as well as freedom from financial stress and opportunities for interesting and enriching experiences. In addition, material possessions, "stuff" as the late comedian George Carlin called it, can fulfill practical, aesthetic, entertainment, athletic, and other needs and wants.

At the same time, the pursuit of wealth and material goods for their own sake or for the belief that they will offer something deeper and more meaningful is, based on extensive research, a fantasy foisted on parents and children alike by popular culture to meet its own profit-driven ends. Materialism refers to "focusing on attaining material possessions" and the belief that the amassing of wealth, "materialistic pursuits, accumulation of things, and presentation of the 'right image'" are necessary for happiness. Popular culture does its best to convince people that wealth and material-ism will make them happier, more attractive, and popular and will boost their social status. Yet research shows that wealth has quite the opposite effect: specifically, people who value high financial success are less happy, have lower self-esteem, are more depressed and anxious, and have less healthy relationships. Despite this evidence, popular culture seems to be winning the battle, and its influence has trickled down to children.

Children these days are inundated by a popular culture that is saturated with messages of wealth and materialism, from celebrity magazines that feature mansions, expensive cars, and start-up millionaires (and even bil-lionaires) in their twenties to reality TV shows featuring ordinary people who get rich with little talent or effort (e.g., *Jersey Shore*). Children get the message early and often that they can distinguish themselves with money and stuff. These messages from popular culture convey to them that wealth and material possessions are not only important but also abso-lutely essential. It's no surprise, then, that a recent survey revealed that 81 percent of young people rate "getting rich" as their first or second most important goal. There is not, however, any accompanying messages about what it actually takes to make money or any discussion of the problems that come from valuing money too much.

Other research indicates that parents, peers, and popular culture most strongly influence children's beliefs about money and material goods. Research has also shown that children's materialism can be predicted by their mothers' materialism (the more materialistic mom is, the more her children are), how involved and nurturing mothers are in their children's lives (the less involved and nurturing moms are, the more materialistic their children are), and children's perceptions of interparent conflict (the more conflict they perceive, the more materialistic they are).

Most of the research on popular culture's impact on whether children come to overvalue wealth and materials has focused on television advertising, and those findings are clear: children who are exposed to more advertising are more materialistic. They also ask their parents to buy more things, and those requests lead to more parent-child conflict. For example, heavy television viewers use the nag factor far more than light television viewers to persuade their parents to buy things they want. Moreover, materialism is negatively related to prosocial values, behavior, and self-esteem.

Fame

A recent study reported findings that are truly alarming—and I think you'll agree. The researchers analyzed the values expressed on the most popular television shows among so-called tweens (children between the ages of nine and eleven) every decade from 1967 to 2007. Just so you can get a sense of how TV viewing has changed, here are the shows that were selected: 1967, *Andy Griffith* and *The Lucy Show*; 1977, *Laverne and Shirley* and *Happy Days*; 1987, *Growing Pains* and *Alf*; 1997, *Sabrina the Teenage Witch* and *Boy Meets World*; 2007, *American Idol* and *Hannah Montana*. The results revealed little change in values presented on the shows between 1967 and 1997, during which time the five most expressed values were community feeling, benevolence, image, tradition, and popularity (three of the five would, in general, be considered healthy). The five least expressed values were fame, physical fitness, hedonism, spiritualism, and financial success (three of five would, in general, be considered unhealthy). Only during the most recent decade did a dramatic shift in values occur. The new top-five values were fame, achievement, popularity, image, and financial success (with self-centeredness and power close behind). The latest bottom-five values were spiritualism, tradition, security, conformity, and benevolence (with community feeling to follow).

An additional analysis of the data revealed a significant increase from 1997 to 2007 in the importance of fame to the main characters in the television shows. Related values that also increased substantially included ambition, comparison to others, attention seeking, conceitedness, glamour, and materialism.

Given that the values did not gradually shift during the decades studied, but rather abruptly changed in the past decade, the results can't readily be attributed to demographic patterns related to increased wealth or education. Instead, the most dramatic change, and the likely cause of these results, is the rapid and all-encompassing emergence of new technology, which has given popular culture new and startling reach and influence.

Programming that expresses these value messages to your children is growing by the year. Since the data from this study were collected, more televisions shows aimed at the tween audience are being produced, including *Glee*, *Big Time Rush*, *True Jackson*, and *iCarly*. In fact, seven of the top ten shows aimed at tweens are about teenagers who have achieved fame with careers in entertainment. Not surprisingly, all these shows send the same message: fame is the singular goal, and it can be achieved with little preparation or hard work.

Of course, you could argue that your children aren't paying attention to popular culture's value messages, much less internalizing them. Unfortunately, preliminary research indicates that children are getting the message from popular culture. According to this new study, fame is now the number-one aspirational value among children nine to eleven years old. Another survey of children younger than ten years found that, among their ten favorite things, being famous, attractive, and rich topped the list, and being fat topped the list of worst things.

Kids 3.0 and Values

So what values will Kids 3.0 need to thrive in the twenty-first century? Perhaps surprisingly, my answer is this: the same values that have enabled children to thrive in previous generations, including respect, responsibility, hard work, integrity, and compassion, just to name a few. The increased presence of popular culture and the burgeoning use of new technology in no way changes that calculus. To the contrary, more than ever, solid values are what will enable Kids 3.0 to stand out from children who become victims of popular culture and technology.

You can, of course, do your best to shield your children from the corrosive values of popular culture by limiting their exposure to popular culture and their use of the latest technology. This attempt will, as they become more immersed in school and the larger social and digital world, become increasingly fruitless. You can't just sit back and play defense when it comes to values. Popular culture is just too powerful and omnipresent. You need to take your values directly to your children.

Unfortunately, many people have lost touch with what values are and their place in their families' lives. They think that values are lofty ideals that have little connection with their daily lives. Yet values should be woven into the very fabric of your family's lives. You can show your children how values are reflected in the activities they participate in, who they interact with, and the choices they make. For example, finishing a school project on time, taking out the garbage, and reading with a younger sibling all express positive values of discipline, responsibility, and caring, respectively.

Again using contrasts as a learning tool, you can show your children how negative values, like laziness, unkindness, and lying, are conveyed. There is no better classroom for teaching about unhealthy values than through its many conduits of technology. Despite your best efforts to protect your children from these destructive values, they will see them on television, on the Internet, and in video games. You can use these teachable moments to highlight healthy and unhealthy values by talking to your children about the messages they're getting through their immersion in popular culture and technology and what underlying values are being communicated. In presenting these value violations, you can explore with them the benefits and costs of following and disregarding healthy values, the short- and long-term consequences of a breach of values, and the choices that they will have to make about values in the future.

Values Are Your Family: Create a Family-Value Culture

Everyone needs and wants to be part of a culture. Belonging to a culture offers people a sense of identity, feelings of connectedness, shared values, and support when faced with the challenges of life. Children will seek out a culture that is most present in their lives and that provides the most rewards. You can protect your children from popular culture by creating a family-value culture—a family environment that expresses the values that your family holds dear—that has an equally powerful, but positive, influence on your children. You must believe deeply in and be wholly committed to your family-value culture, and it should be a walking, talking, feeling, acting, living expression of the values you want your children to learn. You must express your family-value culture in all the ways that I will describe here. A family-value culture that your children are raised in precedes the presence of popular culture and can fill the need for a culture in your children's lives.

Values Are You: Make Sure You
Walk the Walk on Values

For the duration of your children's early years, you are their most powerful influence and role model. Everything you say, feel, and do sends your children subtle, yet influential, messages about your values. Because of this impact, you must ask yourself whether you are walking the walk when it comes to your values.

Conveying values to your children is further complicated by the fact that what you think you are teaching them is not always what they are learning from you. This disconnect can occur because your actions may not always be clear to your children. For example, your children may see you working hard in your career and being well rewarded financially for your efforts. You may believe that the message they are getting is that you work hard because of your passion for your work. But they may actually be getting the message that you work hard because money is important to you. Clearly, two very different values would arise depending on how they interpret your messages. This is why you should not only make sure you're living a life that expresses your values but also periodically ask yourself whether your actions clearly express the values or whether your children could misinterpret them. Also, ask your children what value messages they are getting from you. For example, you can ask them, "Why do you think Daddy [or Mommy] works so hard?"

Values Are Discussions: Talk to Your
Children about Their Values

"Talk to your children" is perhaps the most commonly offered recommendation from parenting experts, yet it may also be the least adopted, particularly when it comes to values. Whether it's a lack of clarity of what their values are or simply a lack of time and energy, research indicates that many parents don't sit down and have this all-important discussion about values.

Talking to your children about values can occur in a spontaneous or structured way. Your family's daily life is filled with value lessons waiting to be taught; having your antenna up for these teaching opportunities allows you to spot them immediately. You can also make value discussions a part of your family-value culture. For example, you might designate one dinner per week to the discussion of a particular value.

Talking with your children about values and your family-value culture also communicates to them that values are important to you and should be important to them. This value education provides children with the foundation with which they can further explore values and adopt healthy values themselves.

Values Are Emotions: Let Your Children Feel Values

Emotions have a persuasive influence on whether children act in value-driven ways. Some experts believe that emotions, such as empathy and guilt, are inborn and serve an adaptive purpose by helping ensure that people behave in ways that benefit themselves, their families, and their communities.

Some emotions restrain children from acting badly. Fear, for example, is a visceral deterrent that makes children uncomfortable when contemplating immoral behavior. Guilt causes feelings of regret and shame after children have violated a value. Because children don't like to feel bad, they are less likely to act against their values again.

Other emotions encourage the expression of certain values. Emotions such as inspiration motivate children to act morally, because they connect valued behavior with these feel-good emotions. When children behave ethically, they experience emotions such as pride and satisfaction, which further reinforce their value-driven behavior.

Values Are Choices: Let Your Children Make Decisions about Values

Values provide a moral compass for children to follow in the choices they face and the decisions they make in their lives. When faced with competing options, for example, whether to lie or tell the truth to their parents, children's values and their related emotions will dictate what value choices they make. Children who understand values and connect positive emotions to those values are more likely to undergo a value-driven decision process—consider their options, weigh the benefits and costs, and make choices consistent with their family-value culture—rather than to make a decision based on self-interest or on urgings from popular culture or peers.

Because values are choices, children must choose the values they want to live by. Creating a family-value culture encourages your children to think critically about their own values and to make decisions about the values they choose to adopt. Recognize that your children will periodically make bad choices and act counter to your own values. Use these opportunities to help your children learn more about their values, why they made a poor decision, and how they can make better choices in the future. For example, if you catch one of your children in a lie, you can ask several useful questions:

- Why did you lie?
- What were the benefits of lying?
- What were the consequences of lying?
- What have you learned from being caught in a lie?

This discussion, accompanied by appropriate punishment (yes, it is essential that they learn that their actions have consequences), helps your children understand why they made a poor choice and see the consequences of the bad decision, and it shows them why they should make better choices in the future.

Values Are Social: Let Your Children Interact with Values

Values are influenced by the reactions that children get from others in response to their behavior. Value-driven behavior that is rewarded with social praise and validation will be internalized. Actions that are in conflict with positive values and are punished socially with disapproval from others will be discarded. A problem is that children are vulnerable to social influence from many sources, including those that are unhealthy. Peer pressure often interferes with children's adopting healthy values. For example, in some schools, children who study hard and have educational goals are ostracized, and those who are slackers are admired. Popular culture exerts a similar influence. Advertising, from products from fast food and soft drinks to clothing and technology, conveys the message that buying certain products will make children popular and winners, and if they don't, losers. Children get messages from popular culture, for example, that they must dress a certain way to be popular. They then impose that "value" on their peers, causing them to either succumb to the pressure and be accepted or deny the pressure and risk rejection.

The pressure to conform and be accepted will grow substantially as your children grow, and they may feel compelled to make choices based on their need for acceptance. Maintaining your influence in the face of increasing opposition from outside social forces is one of your most difficult challenges. Your best defense against this social influence is instilling positive values at an early age and continually exposing your children to positive social messages so that they will recognize bad influences and unhealthy values, and not feel the need to adopt values and act in certain ways just to be accepted.

Values Are Experiences: Let Your Children Encounter Values

The best way to instill values in your children is to immerse them in activities that reflect and express your family-value culture. For example, when your children participate in charitable work, the arts, or sports, you're not telling them that they will be learning about values. Instead, they are experiencing your family's values, interacting with others who share your values, accomplishing goals that are consistent with your values, and experiencing positive emotions connected to those values.

Value-driven experiences are most influential on children when they have to get their hands dirty. For example, although donating money to a charity can certainly teach the value of giving, children aren't able to connect fully with the meaning of those values because they can't see the end result of their actions. In contrast, spending a day in a home for the elderly, for example, connects the value of giving with an immediate beneficial result, thus causing children to feel deep emotions—empathy and kindness—which lie at the heart of children buying into the values.

Values Are Life: Let Your Children Live Values

The real power of values is how they are expressed in the minutiae of your family's daily lives. Anything value related that you do with your children in your family's daily life, for example, doing household chores or reading to your children, is a small but powerful message that communicates your family-value culture to your children:

- Responsibility: when they bring their dishes to the sink after dinner
- Cooperation: getting ready for school on time

- Kindness: helping their younger sibling
- Hard work: practicing the piano regularly
- Compassion: volunteering at a favorite charity

You want to show them that these small acts are actually significant deeds that reflect your family-value culture and are the stuff your family's lives are made of.

Practical Ways to Teach Values

The recommendations that I just offered are broad strokes on the canvas of your children's lives that teach values to them. There are also practical ways they can learn about values from your direct interactions with them.

Set Limits

One down-to-earth way values are expressed is through the rules, boundaries, and expectations that you establish in your family. Each of these prescriptions are value based, and they convey important messages about values. For example, you can limit the amount of unhealthy food your children can eat or allow them to watch television for only one hour a day.

Unfortunately, many children simply see rules, boundaries, and expectations as limitations placed on their freedom by their parents without rationale or purpose. When you explicitly link your values with these directives, you show your children the values behind your dictates (you're not just being an overly strict parent!). Don't just simply lay down the law; rather, explain and discuss with your children how the limits you place on them are related to your values and how they benefit them.

Setting limits has real implications on your children's involvement with popular culture and technology. When you don't allow them, for example, to play violent video games or spend hours with social media, and you also explain to them the rationale behind your decisions, you're communicating to them that you don't value these activities. Your children may not like your decisions, but at least they'll know that you have real reasons for them.

Explain the Consequences of Values

Perhaps the most powerful way to help children understand the importance of values is to show and discuss with them the consequences of healthy and unhealthy values. A valuable lesson for them is that if they act with positive values in mind, good things will happen, and if they act according to bad values, bad things happen. For example, show them that good effort in school results in good grades, being compassionate toward others causes others to respond in kind, and being caught lying results in punishment and a loss of trust.

Unfortunately, acting on good values is not always rewarded, and bad values are not always punished in our society—this can be an obstacle in teaching your children about value consequences. Popular culture often glorifies and rewards bad values. For example, domestic violence, drug use, and other bad behavior don't prevent professional athletes, such as Tiger Woods, or actors, such as Lindsay Lohan, from being given second (and third) chances and being paid exorbitantly. The recording industry persists in promoting hip-hop artists and rock stars despite rap sheets that continue to grow. And, sadly, young people continue to worship them. Your children receive conflicting messages every day, which makes your job of teaching healthy values so much more difficult.

Discuss Value Dilemmas

A powerful way to foster your children's understanding and appreciation of values is to talk to them about the value dilemmas they will face as they move through childhood and into young adulthood. For younger children, topics might include lying, selfishness, stealing, and cheating. Issues for older children can include sexual behavior and alcohol and drug use. You can also identify value breakdowns from popular culture, for example, the poor behavior of actors, athletes, businesspeople, and politicians (there is no shortage of well-known offenders!). This will help them understand that being rewarded despite bad values doesn't justify the values. Moreover, as Tiger Woods learned, there are often significant personal costs to acting on unhealthy values, such as loss of self-respect and admiration from others, as well as lost opportunities.

Value dilemmas arise every day in your children's lives. They may face dilemmas themselves or may see them occur among their peers or in popular culture. You should have your radar attuned to these dilemmas so that you can use them as opportunities to educate your children about these quandaries. With younger children, emphasize the tangible consequences of their decisions, for example, discuss the trouble they would face if they stole a piece of candy they really wanted. With older children, have more sophisticated discussions about self-respect and dangers to themselves and others, and what implications such dilemmas can have on their futures. For example, discuss the personal, social, physical, and criminal ramifications of drinking and driving.

Surround Your Children with Value-Driven People

The omnipresence, intensity, and unrelenting nature of popular culture can be exhausting and discouraging. It can be frustrating to guide your children in the healthy use of technology when the world they're immersed in has ideas to the contrary. You can feel alone against such powerful forces as popular culture and technology.

Fortunately, you aren't alone in your efforts to protect your children from these unhealthy values. I encourage you to actively create a community-value culture that comprises your closest social circle that supports your family-value culture and envelops your children in healthy values. Siblings and extended family members, friends, teachers, coaches, and clergy can all reinforce your value messages and have a significant influence over what your children come to value.

This carefully chosen social world should be an extension of your own values, attitudes, and beliefs and should convey the value messages you want your children to get. You can find like-minded, value-driven people in the community you live in, the schools your children attend, the friends whom you and your children adopt, and the cultural, athletic, religious, and entertainment activities that you and your children participate in.

This support wraps your children in a sort of value-powered force field that can help repel popular culture when your children are outside your home. This shield acts to protect your children by keeping their immediate surroundings, relationships, and messages healthy, even when the larger messages raining down from billboards, stores, television, movies, and the Internet are unhealthy. For example, if you don't like your children to play violent video games, you'll trust that the friends they visit will have a similar attitude.

Building a community of value-driven people means making deliberate choices about the world you want your children to live in away from your home. Ask the following questions:

- Do your children's friends and their parents share your values?
- Does the community you live in support your values?
- Do the schools your children attend reinforce your values?
- Do the activities—cultural, athletic, religious, entertainment—your children participate in encourage your values?

- Do the people and activities in your children's world foster the healthy, life-affirming values, attitudes, and habits that you want your children to develop?

If you answer yes to these questions, then you can feel confident that like-minded people will protect your children when they leave the house. If you answer no to these questions, you should consider how you can surround your children with healthier influences. Small changes can include finding a new sports league that emphasizes fun and participation over winning, a new piano teacher who is less demanding, or making the local mall off limits to your children. Large-scale changes can include enrollment in a new school, attending a different house of worship, or not allowing your children to see friends who you believe are bad influences on them.

When you actively create a caring community, you accrue significant benefits for both you and your children. You'll feel less alone and more supported as you face the behemoth of popular culture and technology. Your children will feel less of a burden to conform to a world that they know isn't healthy for them. When your children leave your home, you and they will know they are entering a world that is populated by like-minded value-driven people who will assist them in making positive choices in the face of unrelenting pressure from popular culture and technology to act otherwise.

Raising Kids 3.0: Values

- List the values you want your children to learn.

- List the values your children are getting from popular culture and technology.

- Compare the two lists and identify discrepancies.

- What limits, expectations, and consequences have you established that communicate healthy values to your children?

- What steps can you take to ensure that your children get your value messages over those of popular culture and technology?

Chapter 7

Thinking: What's on Their Minds?

"I'm doing Facebook, YouTube, having a conversation or two with a friend, listening to music at the same time. I'm doing a million things at once, like a lot of people my age. Sometimes I'll say: I need to stop this and do my schoolwork, but I can't."

—*Vishnal, age seventeen*

Thinking—the capacity to reflect, reason, and draw conclusions on the basis of our experiences, knowledge, and insights. It's what makes us human and has enabled us to communicate, create, build, advance, and become civilized. Thinking encompasses so many aspects of who our children are and what they do, from observing, learning, remembering, questioning, and judging to innovating, arguing, deciding, and acting.

There is also little doubt that all the new technologies, led by the Internet, are shaping the way we think in ways obvious and subtle, deliberate and unintentional, and advantageous and detrimental. The uncertain reality is that, with this new technological frontier in its infancy and developments emerging at a rapid pace, we have neither the benefit of historical hindsight nor the time to examine the value and cost of these advancements in terms of how they influence our children's ability to think.

There is, however, a growing body of research that technology can be both beneficial and harmful to the different ways in which children think. Moreover, this influence isn't just affecting children on the surface of their thinking. Rather, because their brains are still developing and malleable, digital natives' frequent exposure to technology is actually wiring the brain in ways very different from in previous generations. As with advances throughout history, what is clear is that the technology that is available determines how our brains develop and how they function after they are fully developed. For example, as the technology writer Nicholas Carr has observed, the emergence of reading encouraged our brains to be focused and imaginative. In contrast, the rise of the Internet is strengthening our ability to scan information rapidly and efficiently.

The effects of technology on children are complicated, and they have both benefits and costs. Whether technology helps or hurts the development of your children's thinking depends on what specific technology they use and with what frequency. As I have emphasized throughout *Raising Generation Tech*, you have, at least early in their lives, the power to dictate your children's relationship with technology and, as a result, its influence on their thinking, from synaptic activity to conscious thought.

I'm going to focus on the areas that the latest thinking and research has shown to be most influenced by technology: attention, decision making, and memory and learning. Importantly, you can counteract the influence technology has on all these areas.

Attention

Think of attention as the gateway to thinking. Without it, other aspects of thinking, namely, perception, memory, language, learning, creativity, reasoning, problem solving, and decision making, are greatly diminished or can't occur at all. The ability of your children to learn to focus effectively and consistently lays the foundation for almost all aspects of their growth and is fundamental to their development into Kids 3.0.

Attention has been found to be a highly malleable quality and most directly influenced by the environment in which it is used. This selective attention can be found in the animal kingdom in which different species develop attentional skills that help them function and survive. For example, wolves and other predators have highly tuned visual attention that enables them to spot and track their prey. In contrast, their prey have well-developed auditory attention that allows them to hear approaching predators. In both cases, animals' attentional abilities have developed on the basis of the environment in which they live.

The same holds true for human development. Whether infants' recognition of their parents' faces or students paying attention in class, children's immediate environment determines the kind of attention that they develop. In generations past, children directed considerable time to reading, an activity that offered few distractions and required intense and sustained attention, imagination, and memory. The advent of television altered that attention by offering children visual stimuli, the opportunity to divide attention without missing information, and little need for imagination. Then the Internet was invented, and children were thrust into a vastly different environment in which distraction is the norm, consistent attention is impossible, imagination is unnecessary, and memory is inhibited.

One of the most frequent criticisms of early and frequent exposure to technology is that it conditions the brain to pay attention to information very differently than reading. The metaphor that is often used is the difference between scuba diving and riding a Jet Ski. Book reading is like scuba diving; the diver is submerged in a quiet, visually restricted, slow-paced setting with few distractions and, as a result, is required to focus narrowly and think deeply on the limited information that is available. In contrast, using the Internet is like riding a Jet Ski; the rider is skimming along the surface of the water at high speed, exposed to a broad vista, surrounded by many distractions, and able to focus only fleetingly on any one thing.

In fact, studies have shown that those who read uninterrupted text have faster completion and better understanding, recall, and learning than those who read text filled with hyperlinks and ads. Those who read a text-only version of a presentation, as compared to one that included video, found the presentation to be more engaging, informative, and entertaining, a finding contrary to conventional wisdom, to be sure. Also contrary to conventional educational wisdom, research has shown that students who were allowed Internet access during class didn't recall the lecture or perform as well on a test of the material as those who weren't wired during class. Finally, a robust finding indicated that reading develops reflection, critical thinking, problem solving, and vocabulary better than visual media, all essential skills for raising Kids 3.0.

Exposure to technology isn't all bad. Research shows that, for example, video games and other screen media improve visual-spatial capabilities and increase attentional ability, reaction times, and the capacity to identify significant details among clutter. Also, rather than making children stupid, technology may just be making them different from previous generations of children. For example, the ubiquitous use of Internet search engines is causing children to become less adept at remembering things and more skilled at remembering where to find things. Given the ease with which information can be accessed these days, it only stands to reason that knowing where to look is becoming more important for children than actually knowing something. It also has been hypothesized that not having to retain information in our brain allows it to engage in more higher-order processing, such as contemplation, critical thinking, and problem solving.

What does all this mean for raising your children? The bottom line is that too much screen time and not enough other activities, such as reading, playing games, and good old imaginative play, will result in your children having their brains wired in ways that will make them less prepared to thrive in this crazy new world of technology.

Information Overload

The Internet, and all the new computer and communication technology that has sprung from it, has been a boon to the information age, making information instantaneously available at children's fingertips. The sheer volume of information accessible online is staggering; there are around fifty billion pages on the Web. Information continues to become more readily available to children in less time; from websites and email to RSS feeds and Twitter, children have input at an unprecedented rate and volume. This information age is the crazy new world your children are being raised in, and it will likely be a determining factor in how their brains and minds develop.

For all its benefits, a real danger for children in this world that is available at all times is that they will become overwhelmed with this torrent of information. Neuroscientists call this notion cognitive overload, and it occurs when the inflow of information hinders rather than helps the ability to think.

Now let me digress briefly and make an important distinction: accessing information is not thinking. Yes, information is useful, but not necessary, for thinking. Thinking involves what children's brains do with the information, more specifically, perceive, remember, organize, synthesize, reason, create, problem solve, and make decisions based on that information. Raising Kids 3.0 is all about wiring your children's brains and teaching them how to think, not just access information.

This overflow of information affects children in several ways. First, in today's technological world, information is coming at them from many directions, for example, through television, computer, texts, hyperlinks, and on-screen ads. Children are enveloped in an environment of constant information and distraction. As a result, children have neither the time nor the attention spans to actually process the information and use it in productive ways, like learning a subject in school or exploring a topic of personal interest in greater depth.

Second, with children's minds being flooded with information, their primary motivation is not to think about that information but to move the information through their minds as quickly as possible to make room for the next wave of information. Children can use one of two strategies when their inbox starts to overflow. They can ignore the information completely, which means that they won't retain it. The downside here is that they'll need to retain some of the information, for example, the information necessary to pass a test in school. Or children process it quickly to clear their minds for new information flowing in. The problem here is that the output, for example, a paper based on a topic learned in class, will be of poor quality because the information wasn't adequately thought through.

At the heart of the problem with information overload is that such large and never-ending quantities of input interfere with children's ability to engage in "interput," a word I coined to denote the thinking processes from input to output. With so much information coming in and the need to get information out, interput suffers; there is neither the time nor the energy to adequately process all of the information that children receive in this digital world.

Information is only a tool; its value lies in how we use it. The Internet has placed a universe of information at your children's disposal. What makes children Kids 3.0 is not the availability of information but how they use it, in other words, their interput. Only through interput does information become meaningful to children, and only then can it morph from simple data to knowledge, insight, expertise, and wisdom. That comes only when children have time for interput—stopping in the middle of this flood of information to think about, wrestle with, challenge, and build on the information that arrives at their technological doorstep.

For children, information without interput has serious consequences; it means riding a Jet Ski rather than being a scuba diver. The absence of interput prevents children from taking ownership of the information— making it theirs—and not only incorporating it into their information hard drive but also integrating it into their knowledge library. It also keeps them from transforming input from cold and lifeless data into a power plant of insight, creativity, and innovation. It ultimately prevents your children from putting the information into conscious, meaningful, and beneficial action.

On a final note, although technology discourages thinking, this effect is simply a by-product of its use, not an intentional strategy to manipulate children. That cannot, however, be said for popular culture, which actively discourages your children from thinking. Popular culture doesn't want your children to think, or specifically to engage in critical thinking or healthy skepticism. These aspects of thinking result in perspective, moderation, and balance—all qualities that are anathema to popular culture. Instead, popular culture much prefers that children absorb the information they are given, usually in terms of what they should think, feel, and do, and then simply act on it without thought, typically by buying things. By giving your children the space to think, you give them an essential tool for resisting the powerful and omnipresent force of popular culture.

Information for Kids 3.0

So how can you help your children swim against the tide of information overload and find the time for interput? The answer to this question is really quite simple but nonetheless far from easy in this world of 24/7 connectivity. You have to be the spigot that controls the flow and type of information your children get.

Assuming an active role in helping your children manage their flow of information shouldn't be unilateral. What you deem as unimportant may be essential to them. Instead, engage your children in a conversation about information. You may be surprised to learn that your children are acutely aware that the current rate of information that is flooding into their brains is overwhelming and stressing them out. They just don't know how to deal with it, but that's where you come in. Work with your children to find ways in which you can help them to reduce their input to a manageable level without, of course, causing them to miss out on important information.

You can help your children control their flow of information in several ways. First, ask yourself and your children how the amount of information affects them. You will probably see that they feel overwhelmed and uncomfortable with it. They will want your help in managing it better.

Second, ask yourself and your children what purpose all of this input serves them and whether the typical information they receive each day really brings value to their life. Admittedly, you might have to do some negotiating with your children when disagreements arise about what is and isn't important. Both you and your children will probably have to do some negotiating to come to consensus on what information they receive every day, primarily through technology, has value and what is just clutter, like the dozens of text messages they send and receive, the social media updates they scour, and the television programs they watch while doing their homework. I have found, though, that children usually recognize that much of this deluge of information is, in fact, not very important. Then, work with your children to set reasonable limits that will help them feel better and do better in school and in other important activities. Hopefully, this exercise will put your children's flow of information into perspective and show them that much of that input is simply distracting clutter.

With your and your children's new understanding of the importance of interput and with their input load reduced, they can create a space in their lives in which they can absorb the information that is most beneficial to them and have the time to engage in an activity vital for becoming Kids 3.0: thinking. The result for your children? Fewer feelings of being overwhelmed and stressed; more time to devote to important things; more thinking; and better output in their personal, familial, social, and academic lives.

Multitasking

Like many digital natives, your children are probably on their way to becoming lifelong multitaskers. Multitasking involves engaging in two or more activities simultaneously. Your children may be doing their homework, checking their text messages, surfing the Web, and listening to music all at the same time (or so they think). Why do they multitask? The short answer is because they can, and it's what just about every young person does these days. As the research I described in chapter 2 indicates, children these days spend about seven and a half hours a day interacting with technology unrelated to school, and when multitasking is counted, that number jumps to an astonishing ten and three-quarter hours.

There's one problem with this scenario: there is no such thing as multitasking—at least not in the way you may think of it. The fact is that multitasking, as most people understand it, is a myth that has been promulgated by the technological-industrial complex to make everyone feel more competent, efficient, productive, and—well—cool.

Real multitasking involves engaging in two tasks simultaneously. Here's the catch, though. It's only possible if two conditions are met: (1) at least one of the tasks is so well learned that it's automatic, meaning that no focus or thought is necessary to engage in the task (e.g., walking, eating) and (2) both tasks involve different types of brain processing. For example, children can study effectively while listening to classical music because reading comprehension and processing instrumental music engage different parts of the brain. However, the ability to retain information while reading and listening to music with lyrics declines significantly because both tasks activate the language center of the brain.

Your children, in this case, are actually task switching. Rather than engaging in several tasks simultaneously, they are, in fact, shifting from one task to another to another. For example, they switch from their telephone conversation to their homework assignment to a text message to a newly opened hyperlink on their computer screen and back to their assignment in the belief that they're doing everything simultaneously, but they're not.

Research has uncovered two findings that are at odds with the conventional wisdom about so-called multitasking. A summary of studies examining multitasking describes how multitasking is neither effective nor efficient. These findings have demonstrated that when your children shift focus from one task to another, that transition is neither fast nor smooth. Instead, there is a lag time during which the brain must yank itself from the initial task and then glom onto the new task. This shift, though it feels instantaneous, takes time. In fact, up to 40 percent more time is needed to complete a task as compared to single tasking.

A 2010 study offers perhaps the most surprising result: those who consider themselves great multitaskers are in fact the worst multitaskers. Those who rated themselves as chronic multitaskers made more mistakes, could remember fewer items, and took longer to complete a variety of focusing tasks analogous to multitasking than those self-rated as infrequent multitaskers. Other research has found that children perform worse on their homework if it is done while watching TV.

The level of distraction that students encounter when simultaneously working on their computers and watching television is startling. A study tracked students' eye movements and found that, during a half-hour period, people switched their attention between their computer and television 120 times. Amazingly, the participants in the study weren't aware of how distracted they were, guessing that they looked back and forth only about fifteen times in thirty minutes. Even more astonishing, the median length of time that people looked at television and their computer was two and six seconds, respectively. Given this level of distraction, I wonder how children ever learn or get anything done while studying.

Still another study found that a sample of middle school, high school, and university students lost focus every three minutes during a fifteen-minute study period on their computers. Not surprisingly, these distractions were directly related to the number of windows (e.g., Facebook, instant messaging, web pages) that students had open on their computers. Further analyses revealed that children's ability to stay on task was highly predictive of good grades. In addition, the best predictors of poor grades were a tendency to multitask, the total number of hours each day children spent with technology, and whether they checked their Facebook pages at least once every fifteen minutes. How widespread is this phenomenon? A survey found that 73 percent of college students can't study without some form of technology, and 38 percent can't last ten minutes without checking their technology.

Understanding Multitasking

What does this mean for your children who are growing up in a world in which multitasking not only is the norm but also is considered essential for success (and social acceptance)? Well, it means that your children don't really multitask. Despite appearances, your children simply can't talk on the telephone, read text messages, and watch YouTube videos all at the same time. In fact, when your children think they're cruising along the information highway, the research I just described shows that they're actually stepping on the gas then hitting the brakes, over and over again.

Consider how children did homework before the advent of the radio and television. They would have an assignment they needed to complete, so they would stop what they were doing, for example, playing with friends, and move to the desk in their room or to the dining room table to focus on their homework. The most distraction children would experience might be someone entering the room. The very primitiveness and infrequency of these distractions enabled children to stay focused on their homework for extended periods and to get it done quickly and well.

With the introduction of the radio and television into the home, the occurrence of multitasking increased as did the distractions that children who were attempting to study experienced. But these distractions were relatively minor compared to those of today, and because children rarely had radios and televisions in their rooms, parents could easily monitor and limit them.

Now let's fast-forward a generation to the present. Children's ability to immerse themselves in a single activity is becoming a lost art. New technology, in the form of mobile phones, email, texting, the Internet, and more specifically Twitter, Facebook, and other social media, keeps children in a constant state of distraction. Moreover, children can use all this technology in the privacy of their own bedrooms, which makes it more difficult for parents to supervise these activities. The result is less attention paid to their homework, more time needed for its completion, and in all likelihood lower-quality work.

Single Tasking for Kids 3.0

Hopefully, you're now convinced that multitasking isn't what it purports to be and definitely doesn't do your children any favors. Your next step is to show them (and perhaps yourself) how to single task. The answer is definitely not rocket science; it simply requires your children to make deliberate choices about what they wish to focus on and to maintain that single focus until the task is completed. The bad news is that it can be difficult for children to break multitasking habits that may have become ingrained. The good news is that, with some commitment and discipline, your children can retrain those habits and, in a relatively short time, experience the clear benefits of becoming comfortable and adept single taskers.

Single tasking starts with looking for ways to maximize your children's ability to focus and minimize their potential distractions. Given that single tasking may involve some pretty significant changes in your children's use of technology, I would encourage that you collaborate with them so they have buy-in on the changes you implement.

First focus on your children's approach to completing homework to help them shift from multitasking to single tasking. If they're like many children, they probably do their homework in the living room or family room at your house. This may mean that there is a lot of distracting activity going on around them, such as you doing chores or their siblings coming and going. So, the first step is to find them a quiet space they won't be interrupted in. Your first thought might be their bedroom; although it's quiet, it probably offers your children even more distractions when they get tired, bored, or stuck on an assignment. A den or study, if available, is a better option.

Second, help them get comfortable and organized. They should ideally sit in a chair that's comfortable—but not too comfortable. Sofas and beds are just asking for daydreaming or napping. Their workspace should allow them easy access to whatever they need for their homework and should be uncluttered (clutter equals distraction).

Third, and most important, have them put away distracting technology. This means no mobile phones (just having them in sight will be a distraction), no social media (if your children are too tempted, there's software that can give you control), no television (old school, but still a huge distraction), and only instrumental music (for reasons noted earlier). If they need to use a computer for their homework, you can disable Internet access. You don't want these changes to seem harsh to your children (and they will be if they're accustomed to multitasking), so allow them breaks to check their text messages, update their Facebook pages, or call a friend.

My experience has been that children usually offer initial resistance to this shift from distracted multitasking to focused single tasking, particularly if they're used to the former. If you can at least convince them to try it out for, say, two weeks, and perhaps even offer them incentives (research shows that bribery to initiate behavior change is effective), then you create the time to retrain their habits, allow them to become comfortable with the changes, and most important, see the benefits. Your children will find that single tasking is effective—they're able to focus better, learn more, and do better in school. They'll also find it more efficient, as it gives them more time to do the things they want, such as use the technology that was missing while they were single tasking.

Decision Making

Decision making is another aspect of children's thinking that seems to be suffering as a result of the latest technology. This poor decision making is illustrated by events over the past few years involving young people making egregiously bad decisions that involve technology (not to mention the frequent examples occurring in the adult world!): teens' sext messages have been released in cyberspace, embarrassing or illegal behavior has been recorded on mobile phones and broadcast on YouTube, and cyberbullying has provoked tragic consequences.

In looking at children's decision-making process, let me begin with a brief lesson in brain anatomy and functioning. Children start off at a severe disadvantage when it comes to decision making because, as I've discussed previously, the prefrontal cortex doesn't fully develop until well past adolescence. The prefrontal cortex is instrumental in executive functioning, namely determining good from bad, planning, recognizing future consequences, predicting outcomes, and suppressing socially inappropriate behavior. This means that children begin their lives behind the curve when it comes to decision making; their default is to make poor decisions. So, anything that encourages children to make bad decisions just adds insult to injury.

Let's start by putting bad decisions in their proper historical context. Humans have been prone to flawed decision making for as long as we have roamed the earth. Whether a mild act of embarrassing stupidity, such as putting one's foot in one's mouth with an untoward comment, or an act of career-ending idiocy, such as insulting the boss around the water cooler, faulty decision making is a decidedly human attribute.

Why have we not evolved into better decision makers after so many eons of bad decisions? Because we have yet to gain mastery over our primal urges or our unconscious needs and insecurities, both of which are the primary drivers of poor decisions. Nor, as the psychological sciences have shown us, have we been able to avoid falling prey to the myriad cognitive biases (e.g., selective attention, rationalization) that blur our lenses of reason. All these forces conspire to prevent us from gathering sufficient information, analyzing it effectively, and using it exclusively to come to "rational" decisions (in other words, we will never be like *Star Trek*'s Mr. Spock). Everything that I've just described about all people goes double for children.

Before technological advances, there was time for children to avoid ill-advised decision making. For example, when a teenage boy was angry at the girl who just broke up with him, he had to write the imprudent letter, put it in an envelope, address it and place it in the mailbox, and wait for the mail carrier to arrive. There was, as a result, ample time for him to reconsider the suitability of that particular course of action. Because of the slowness of communication in those primitive days of snail mail, children had the opportunity to, for example, calm down, reflect on their situation, consider the consequences, change their minds, prevent bad behavior, and avoid potential embarrassment, disgrace, or criminal charges. Plus, the blast area, so to speak, was limited by the still-unsophisticated means of communicating those poor decisions to the world (think dynamite).

The technological developments of the past decade have made poor decision making easier and more immediately and widely consequential. Technology discourages children from thinking and deliberation, and it promotes them in acting on their most base impulses, emotions, and needs, such as anger, fear, or need for approval. Children can make regrettable decisions more quickly, be caught in badly conceived acts more readily, and be publicly humiliated before a far broader audience than ever before. Returning to my rejection example, that entire breakup and poorly thought-out reaction can now occur in a matter of seconds, with fewer than 140 characters, and can subsequently be broadcast to millions in a matter of minutes. Making horrendous decisions has never been easier or faster for children. The immediate and collateral damage can be staggering in comparison (think five-hundred-megaton nuclear bomb).

With the emergence of the Internet, email, mobile phones with cameras, Facebook, YouTube, Twitter, gossip websites, and online sleuths, there are newer, faster, and more creative ways to have dreadful decision making illuminated for anyone with an Internet connection to see. Plus, these decisions have a much-longer shelf life because of the digital fingerprints that they leave and that are so difficult to erase. What do the many recent examples of uninspired decision making in this high-tech era have in common? Opportunity, ease, speed, reach, and irreversibility.

Don't think that popular culture is going to get off lightly when it comes to decision making. To the contrary, although technology can cause children to make bad decisions by the very nature of its design, it can't be blamed for those poor decisions. With popular culture, it's an entirely different story. Popular culture wants your children to make flawed decisions because what is usually bad for them is good (profitable) for popular culture.

In fact, popular culture wants to take your children's decisions out of their—and your—hands and assume control over those decisions. Popular culture wants to decide how your children think and feel and how they should act. More specifically, popular culture wants to decide for your children what they wear, what they eat and drink, what television and movies they watch, what video games they play, what music they listen to, and what magazines they read. In other words, popular culture wants to dictate how your children spend their money or yours. To that end, popular culture aims to create children who are impulsive, demanding, greedy, and selfish—and bad decision makers.

Both you and your children can learn important lessons from these popular culture-induced and technology-encouraged poor decisions. For your children, they usually learn the lessons after the fact, when the damage is already done. Sadly, such bad decisions can haunt children's lives for many years to come. For you, the lessons involve ensuring that your children don't have unlimited and unguided access to the popular culture and technology that can aid and abet poor decisions. Perhaps more important, they mean proactively teaching your children how to make good decisions and, in doing so, accelerating the development of the immature prefrontal cortex that is ultimately at fault for the bad decisions.

Decision Making for Kids 3.0

Good decision making is one of the most powerful skills your children need to learn to navigate the crazy new world of popular culture and technology. I promise you, it is not a skill that will develop readily on its own, particularly for digital natives. You should teach your children why popular culture and technology can cause them to make poor decisions and guide them in learning how to make good decisions.

Making Bad Decisions

Whenever I speak to a group of young people, I ask them how many have ever made a bad decision. With complete unanimity and considerable enthusiasm, they all raise their hands. When I then ask whether they will ever make a poor decision in the future, the response is equally fervent. I also ask them why they make less-than-stellar decisions. Their responses include the following:

- I didn't stop to think.
- It seemed like fun at the time.
- I was bored.
- Peer pressure.

- I didn't consider the consequences.
- To get back at my parents.

Yet when I ask them if the faulty decision was worth it, most usually say, "Not really." What this means is that there was glitch in their decision-making program—somewhere between input and output—that caused the bad decision. Because children lack experience and perspective, and, as I noted earlier, because their prefrontal cortex isn't fully developed, they tend to make decisions that are egocentric, rash, and shortsighted. Without forethought, children fail to consider all available information, to engage in a complete cost-benefit analysis, and to think about their long-term consequences.

Let me make a bold statement: children should make poor decisions. Making ill-advised decisions and experiencing the consequences helps your children learn how to make better decisions in the future. A problem arises, however, if their poor decision making continues. Because decision making is a skill, children can become very good at making ill-advised decisions; the more children do anything, good or bad, the better they get at it. The more skillful they become at making regrettable decisions, the more bad decisions they are likely to make in the future. Of course, the long-term personal, social, and professional implications of being poor decision makers are profound, negative, and, I think, obvious.

Learning to Make Good Decisions

Begin by educating your children about the process of making good decisions. The first step, given that children are notorious for acting without thinking, is to teach them to stop before they leap. With a few seconds of hesitation, your children can avoid making flawed decisions. Help your children by catching them in the act, which means that when you see them about to jump without thinking, stop them and guide them through the decision-making process. Also, because you can't always be looking over their shoulder, when they do leap without thinking (and things don't turn out that well), ask them how they could have made a different decision in hindsight.

The next step is to teach your children to think before they act. There are several important questions your children should ask themselves when making a choice. First, "Why do I want to do this?" Children should understand what motivates their decisions, which is challenging because they often face conflicting motivations. They may know that a decision is bad, but they may, for example, feel peer pressure to do it anyway. Except for the most mature children, if decisions come down to doing what is right or what is popular, many children will choose the latter. Because of the ubiquity of popular culture and the omnipresence of technology, forces that push them down the road of a poor decision have never been stronger.

Second, they should ask themselves, "What are my options?" Children often have several possible choices in any given situation. For example, when faced with the possibility of stealing candy from a store with friends, children could (1) take the candy, (2) not take the candy but ignore the fact that their friends are stealing, or (3) try to convince their friends that stealing is wrong. If you've raised your children with healthy values (see chapter 6), they will know what the right decision is. At the same time, they still have to weigh what is right with how it will affect their relationship with their friends.

A third question they should ask is, "What are the consequences of my actions?" (or in their language, "How much trouble will I get into?"). Your children need to judge the risks and rewards of their decisions. The problem is that children often underestimate the costs and overestimate the benefits of their decisions (this is actually a cognitive bias that adults also fall prey to). How your children answer this question will depend on the expectations and consequences you establish for them. If you instill the wrath of God in your children, they're going to weigh those consequences more heavily in their decisions.

Fourth, a question that children can have a difficult time considering is, "How will my decision affect others?" Because children are naturally egocentric, they may not even think about who else their decision is influencing. Teaching your children to ask this question can help them step away from their egocentrism and increase their awareness of others. It can also help them to take others into consideration and make decisions that are beneficial to both themselves and others.

Finally, perhaps the most important question children need to ask themselves is, "Is this decision in my best interests in the long run?" Discussing your children's long-term best interests with them is a valuable way to sensitize them to the conflicts that often arise between short-term gains and long-term benefits. Understanding what is in their best interests in the long run and having those concerns outweigh competing immediate interests is the culmination of the decision-making process.

Coach Good Decision Making

You can help your children learn good decision-making skills by coaching them through decisions. Help them answer the key questions I offered here and take thoughtful steps to the decision. After the decision, help them judge the quality of the decision and, if the decision turned out to be a poor one, what they can learn from it in the future.

You can also present your children with hypothetical situations that they're likely to face, such as a moral dilemma about lying to a friend, and engage them in a conversation about how they would make a decision. Of course, children won't always make deliberate decisions—particularly when they're young—but if you coach them and give them experience with good decision making, they'll use their skills more as they gain maturity.

Raise Good Decision Makers

Ceding decision making to your children is an incremental process based on their age, maturity, and decision-making history. It would be downright dangerous to give children complete latitude in their decision making. You can, however, begin to teach decision making to very young children by setting reasonable limits to their decisions. For example, if you took your children into a convenience store and told them they can have anything they wanted, they would be overwhelmed by the choices (which, research shows, either tend to prevent people from making decisions or result in poor decisions). However, you can give them limited options to choose from, such as jawbreakers, licorice, and bubble gum (or, better yet, sesame sticks, fruit wraps, and yogurt peanuts) and they would then decide which treat they want. Your children will learn to make decisions, but they won't be inundated by the huge number of options available to them.

As your children get older, you can expand the number of choices you give them and then increase the importance of the decisions they can make, for example, allowing them to decide which extracurricular activities they want to participate in or when they decide to go to bed. With each decision, they should recognize and take responsibility for the consequences of those decisions. Also, you should retain veto power when needed but use it judiciously.

Mindfulness

I don't want you to get the wrong idea with this section of *Raising Generation Tech*; I'm no Zen master, and I don't expect parents to teach their children to meditate all day. At the same time, mindfulness is much more than an Eastern or Buddhist philosophy. In fact, it has tremendous significance for children growing up in this crazy new world of popular culture and technology.

Mindfulness is typically thought of in two ways. First, it is the ability to focus completely and nonjudgmentally on the immediate experience at hand. Second, mindfulness involves embracing an attitude of openness, acceptance, curiosity, and novel thinking. Quite simply, being mindful allows us to fully experience whatever we are doing and to gain the complete benefits of what the experience has to offer.

It isn't a stretch to see that popular culture and technology are the antithesis of mindfulness. Both are decidedly not in the self or in the moment. Popular culture is highly judgmental, revering those who are the most beautiful, who are famous, or who have the most money. It is also aspirational: figures in popular culture focus on what they've lacked in the past and what they want to have in the future. Children absorb these messages and do the same, which is anything but mindful.

Technology is all about the constant flow of information and being connected with others. Mobile phones, texting, and social media are sending children a nonstop stream of information; thus, they focus on these messages that are accumulating rapidly in their mental inbox.

Children are also forced to focus on the future and how they're going to send the information that is rapidly building up in their outbox. Social media adds to this burden by drawing children's focus away from themselves and the social world around them. As I noted in chapter 5, social media forces them to assume an external point of reference for themselves. Children have little opportunity to step away from this barrage of information and comparison. This constant pull from the past, the future, and the outside world puts children in a hypervigilant and stressful state.

As I indicated earlier, it also prevents children from focusing on the present, where they can ponder, process, and problem solve.

Children need moments when they can just be. In the frenetic life of popular culture and 24/7 connectivity, children can feel overwhelmed by the onslaught of information directed at them. They need to be able to turn off the fire hose of information periodically to sit quietly with themselves; in other words, they need to be able to mindful.

Between the unlimited exposure to popular culture and technology and the often nonstop, overscheduled lives that so many children lead these days, there is little opportunity for them to ever experience anything that approximates a Zen-like mindfulness or calm. As emerging research is demonstrating, it's very likely that the seeking and reward centers of your children's brains are going bonkers and have little respite. This constant, intense brain activity takes its toll on children, both physically and psychologically.

In this extreme state, children are missing out on the developmentally healthy and recuperative benefits of mindfulness. They aren't able to fully absorb themselves in the moment, whether reading a book, engaging in imaginary play, or going for a hike in the woods, which means that they don't get to fully experience all the great stuff that these opportunities provide. Children aren't allowed to rest their minds and bodies or to recharge their psychic batteries. They also aren't able to learn the practice of deep immersion in the present, which offers benefits in many aspects of their lives, from basic well-being and relationships to achievement in school, sports, and the performing arts. Importantly, children miss out on the ephemeral yet richly satisfying feeling of joy that can come only from being totally engaged in an experience.

Mindfulness shouldn't be relegated to being an Eastern philosophy that has few benefits in our everyday lives. Rather, research conducted over the past three decades has demonstrated profound physical and psychological benefits. Studies have reported more positive emotions; greater resilience to bad experiences; reduced stress, anxiety, and depression; improved immune system activity; and an increased sense of well-being following a regimen of mindfulness exercises.

Recent research has reported that when people are focused on a task they indicate that they have a greater sense of well-being than when their mind wanders. Distractions prevent this state of flow and, as the recent evidence suggests, actually make us less happy. The growth of technology in the past decade has increased the frequency and intensity of these distractions.

Why are children attracted to distraction? I don't think it's attraction but rather an unintended consequence of this recent onrush of technology. As digital natives, your children are simply adapting to the wired world they live in; they're surrounded by technology and people who are using it, so they have little choice but to join in. This immersion in technology, encouraged by their social worlds and frequently not limited by their parents, has forced children to develop attitudes, expectations, behavior, and habits that aren't good for them. In addition, as other research has demonstrated, continuous connectivity produces neurochemical activity in the human brain akin to drug use and gambling.

Not only does technology appear to interfere with your children's happiness—even worse, in their always-connected, constantly distracted lives, children may not learn what real happiness is and where it comes from. Children have come to mistake stimulation, momentary pleasure, and that neurochemical high gained from being always connected for real happiness, which, research indicates, actually comes from meaningful relationships, valued goals, and, yes, absorption in an activity.

Paradoxically, other emerging research indicates that people can become deeply absorbed in technology, like video games and social media, spending hours undistracted and fully focused. As I just mentioned, this concentration appears to occur due to the neurochemical buzz that new technology offers rather than the mindful focus that occurs when children are wrapped in—and enrapt with—life.

Research is demonstrating that because children are so vulnerable to the constant distractions around them, technology may be causing them to lose their ability to absorb themselves in activities such as reading for extended periods. This development has obvious implications for academic and, later, professional performance and productivity. At a more transcendental level, this lost ability may prevent children from learning to find delight in the minutiae of life: the subtlety of the written language found in a book, the smell of lilacs while out for a walk, the sight of a hummingbird extracting nectar from a flower, the intellectual and emotional enjoyment of a stimulating conversation. Without these simple pleasures, perhaps the most profound loss is that of the depth of happiness that can come only from unmediated, complete, and sublime engagement in life.

So consider this: as a parent you want to prevent your children from engaging in activities that make them both less productive and more unhappy. Yet that is precisely what happens when you give your children license to multitask or use technology in a way that prevents them from focusing on the task at hand and interferes with their ability to focus intently for extended periods of time.

Mindfulness for Kids 3.0

In the crazy new world of popular culture and technology, what a wonderful lifelong gift you give your children when you help them to—paraphrasing a well-known adage from the 1960s counterculture movement—turn off and tune in. You do this by creating regular opportunities for your children to disengage from popular culture and technology.

Start by looking at the times when your children are mindless, or the times when they're overwhelmed by information, distracted, and drawn outside of themselves. You will likely find that this state of mind dominates their daily lives.

Next, look for times in your children's days when they have opportunities to be mindful but aren't. Examples include when they're doing their homework, eating meals, walking outside, exercising, or just having family time.

Then, work with your children to help them create situations in which they can be mindful. You might not even want to use the word *mindful*, as it carries connotations that might make the situations seem boring to your children. Instead, you can talk to them about being present, focused, and fully engaged in whatever they're doing, and you can describe the many benefits being present has to offer. For example, explain to your children how multitasking is both ineffective and inefficient while studying, and, as I discussed earlier in this chapter, help your children avoid multitasking while doing their homework. You can also have a rule banning any media, phone calls, or text messages during certain family activities such as dinner.

You can also create family opportunities that allow for and reinforce the value of mindfulness; for example, you can institute a no-technology day each weekend, organize deeply off-the-grid events such as camping trips, or read uninterrupted with your children. Importantly, you want to role model mindfulness by practicing it in your own life, so apply the same exercises that I just described to yourself.

Taking active steps to create mindfulness in the lives of your entire family is a win-win-win situation. Your children learn to be in the moment and are, as a result, more successful in school and extracurricular activities and are overall happier people. By being more mindful yourself, you will be a better person, spouse, and parent. Finally, your family will be less stressed, more harmonious, and more fully engaged in being a family.

Raising Kids 3.0: Thinking

- Identify the ways in which your children's thinking is influenced by the popular culture and technology they are immersed in.

- What steps can you take to limit the amount of multi-tasking you and your children engage in?

- What bad decisions have your children made that could be connected to their involvement with popular culture and technology?

- What steps can you take to teach your children good decision making?

- What can you do to make mindfulness a part of your family's daily lives?

Chapter 8

Relationships: How Connected Are They?

"I'm in the seventh grade. I'm thirteen. I'm not a cheerleader. I'm not the president of the student body. Or captain of the debate team. I'm not the prettiest girl in my class. I'm not the most popular girl in my class. I'm just a kid. I'm a little shy. And it's really hard in this school to impress people enough to be your friend if you're not any of those things. But I go on these really great vacations with my parents between Christmas and New Year's every year. And I take pictures of places we go. And I write about those places. And I post this on my Xanga. Because I think if kids in school read what I have to say and how I say it, they'll want to be my friend."

—Vivien, age thirteen

Popular culture and technology are redefining the meaning of relationships: what relationships are, how they develop and are maintained, and how many relationships we can have. Popular culture, for example, suggests that love can be found in a few weeks on shows like *The Bachelor*, that real family lives mirror the lives featured on shows such as *Kate Plus 8* and the *Real Housewives* franchise, and that friendships and school life are like those on Nickelodeon.

In turn, technology has enabled people who have never met or will never meet to call themselves friends, and the line among connections, acquaintances, and real friends has become blurred with social media like Facebook. We have entered a new era of relationships in which the rules and practices that have guided the development, maintenance, and termination of relationships for eons are being rewritten. Children are learning all about their relationships with their family, friends, and others in this crazy new world of relationships.

It's so important to recognize these changes because relationships play such a central role in who your children become and the quality of the lives they lead. Relationships provide children with a foundation of values, love, security, and support. They are essential in the establishment of children's self-esteem and attitude toward others. Children's early relationships are the template for their future relationships The relationships that children establish early in their lives become the safe harbors from which they can explore their ever-expanding world. Later relationships with peers, teachers, and other influential people shape children's beliefs about the world and the direction that their lives will take. Also, as ample research has demonstrated, relationships are the single greatest predictor of happiness. In fact, every aspect of children's lives is touched by their relationships.

Yet because popular culture and technology are omnipresent in most children's lives, both are shaping how children perceive, feel about, and develop relationships, without their adequately considering the impact that they have on these relationships. Because of popular culture and technology's growing influence on children's relationships, it's incumbent on you to really understand where your children are learning about relationships and whether the information they're absorbing is healthy enough to lay the groundwork for a future filled with positive and life-affirming relationships.

Think of it this way. Do you want your children to learn about the meaning of love from *The Bachelor*, about families from *Keeping Up with the Kardashians*, or about friendship from *Gossip Girl*? Do you want your children to have one hundred Facebook "friends," learn about sex from pornography websites, or experience cyberbullying through instant messages? I'm going to assume that the answer to all of these questions is an emphatic no. Ensuring that your children develop healthy attitudes toward relationships is a fundamental contributor to raising Kids 3.0.

Popular culture offers few healthy benefits in terms of children's relationships. Most messages children get about relationships while watching television shows or movies or while reading celebrity magazines are entirely out of touch with the reality of their relationships; for example, children mistakenly equate popularity with friendship and come to believe the quantity of friendships is more important than quality. Also, time spent engaged in popular culture is time not spent engaged in building real-life relationships.

Nevertheless, many changes in relationships instigated by technology have been positive and productive. Online communities based around shared passions and ideas are a vital wellspring of information and action. Causes have been fomented and movements launched through the Internet. New technology has enabled formerly disconnected people to establish relationships that have increased creativity, innovation, productivity, and efficiency.

On a more personal level, children become acquainted with others on social networking sites before building real friendships offline. Technology has also been a boon to maintaining already-established relationships. If your children have family or friends who live at a great distance, they no longer have to rely on the telephone or snail mail to stay connected. They can be in constant contact through email, texting, Facebook, Flickr, Skype, and Twitter. Tech-savvy grandparents love how technology has enabled them to stay more connected to their grandchildren who live far away.

As with all value-neutral advancements, there are benefits and costs, positive uses and unhealthy misuses, intended outcomes and unintended consequences. My concern is with how children come to define relationships and the role that popular culture and technology play in that process. For example, I hear many young people talking about all the friends they have made on the Web. There's no doubt that the Web has enabled people everywhere to connect and communicate like never before, but I would argue that connection alone doth not a relationship make.

Are Online Relationships Real?

Just as with the use of the old-school term *virtual reality*, many people in technology-based relationships have virtual relationships, yet they consider them real relationships. Virtual relationships feature qualities of real relationships, such as connectedness, communication, and sharing, but they lack missing essential elements that make real relationships, well, real— namely three dimensionality, facial expressions, voice inflection, clear emotional messages, gestures, body language, physical contact, and pheromones.

Online relationships are based on limited information and, as a result, are incomplete; you can know people online, but you know only so much. When connecting with others through technology, you get bits and pieces of people—words on a screen, two-dimensional images, or an electronically transmitted voice—as if you have some, but not all, of the puzzle pieces. You get a picture of them, but you lack enough pieces to get a complete picture. Don't forget that this incomplete puzzle goes both ways.

As I discussed in chapter 5, research has shown that social media users tend to present themselves online in ways that are, at a minimum, slightly more positive impressions of their true selves and, at a maximum, entirely distorted and aggrandized self-representations. This impression management is much easier to do online because recipients of the information aren't in a position to reality test what they see and read. Such misrepresentations don't work as well in real life, and they are not likely to be beneficial to your children as they develop relationships beyond cyberspace.

There are several problems with this common online practice. First, it prevents children from acknowledging and accepting that they are imperfect beings like everyone else. Nor can they learn that, despite their flaws, they are still good people worthy of being valued and liked. Intentionally or otherwise, these misrepresentations are dishonest—not generally a quality that parents want to see in their children.

As relationships develop online, this practice prevents information receivers from making reasoned judgments about the kind of relationship they want with the information sender. Interestingly enough, this practice may also deter the information sender from pursuing a real relationship, because then he or she would be discovered to be an imposter. It doesn't seem unreasonable to assume that children's online misrepresentations would find their way into the early stages of real relationships, when everyone wants to create a good first impression. Yet this inaccurate information would be easily discovered and could hurt or end burgeoning relationships.

The brevity of online communication also mitigates the development of deep relationships. Most forms of social networking, for example, Facebook, Twitter, and texting, involve short and frequent communications that simply don't provide the platform for the rich sharing of thoughts and emotions, which happen to be the superstructure of relationships.

In addition to the concerns I've just expressed, the simple calculus of life is that time spent online in virtual relationships is time not spent in real relationships. This lack of engagement in real relationships can hurt your children's ability to develop healthy relationships in the future. Think of it this way: relationships arise through experience and require certain skills, for example, reading facial expressions, interpreting voice inflection, and feeling empathy. If your children are missing out on flesh-and-blood relationships because they spend so much time online, then they are also missing out on opportunities to learn about and practice the skills that promote healthy relationships.

It's probably no coincidence that the dramatic rise in narcissism and decline in empathy over the past few decades has occurred alongside the rise of the information age and young people's devotion to online pursuits. Of course, your children engage in real relationships at home, at school, and in their other activities, but perhaps not as much as you think. Because children spend more than seven and a half hours a day interacting with non-school-related technology on average, they may actually be spending less time in real relationships than you may believe—and far less time than children in previous generations. That is time in which children are not developing relationship skills nor learning how to maintain healthy relationships. So, in a sense, children these days have less time to practice relationships; with less practice, they are going be less skilled at them.

These limitations don't mean that children should avoid virtual relationships; they can serve a valuable purpose in children's personal and academic lives. The concern is that, with so much time spent online, children substitute virtual relationships for real ones. Unguided and unfettered virtual relationships may come to dominate their relationship universe rather than being just a small subset of their relationships. For example, I often see groups of teenagers sitting together texting rather than talking. I wonder if they're texting one another!

The Attraction of Online Relationships

So why are children attracted to online relationships? On the plus side, social networking allows children to stay in regular touch with their friends, which is particularly important for children who don't see one another in school every day. Cyberspace can act as a meeting place for new friends that then transfer to actual social interactions. Online relationships can help children get beyond the ill ease that can occur when they first meet by allowing them to get to know one another before they meet in person. They are also a way for children who are shy or socially anxious to practice their people skills and gain comfort with new friends before they use those skills in flesh-and-blood relationships.

Interestingly, as one noted researcher, Dr. Danah Boyd, points out, "Children's ability to roam has basically been destroyed…Letting your child out to bike around the neighborhood is seen as terrifying now, even though by all measures, life is safer for kids today." The Internet allows children to "meet up" online and to do the things that children of previous generations could do face to face: talk, gossip, share, joke, flirt, try out new ways of being who they are. The Internet has become the only place children these days are allowed to hang out without their parents' presence or supervision.

Online relationships may provide children with a bubble of safety, comfort, connection, and self-worth in a crazy new world where these attributes are often lacking. We live in a society in which families are no longer nuclear, communities are fragmented, and children can feel isolated and disenfranchised. A popular culture that venerates bad boys and mean girls can create feelings of alienation and anxiety. Fears of inadequacy, rejection, and failure, heightened by a popular culture that reveres perfection, popularity, and success, add to the maelstrom of personal angst that children can feel as they explore relationships. Children who are thrown into this cauldron without adequate support can feel compelled to stay in the comfort of their own room and connect with people safely through their computer.

The reality is that children can fulfill their needs for connection, affiliation, and affirmation through virtual relationships, however limited and ultimately unhealthy that route may be. In doing so, they can come to believe that their needs for friendship and intimacy can be met online without all of the risks and messiness of real-world relationships. The problem is that the absence of messiness in children's online relationships early in their lives also precludes them from learning how to deal with the untidiness that they are certain to face as they establish real relationships in adolescence and adulthood. It also keeps children from experiencing the deep benefits of fully realized relationships that can exist only offline.

Two Keys to Relationships

Selflessness and empathy are two essential ingredients to healthy relationships. Selflessness is the capacity to place others' concerns appropriately ahead of our own. It allows others to sense that, whatever we do, their interests will be considered. Empathy, as I discussed in chapter 5, is the ability to understand another person's perspective and emotions, in other words, to feel what that person feels. Empathy guides our moral behavior toward others; we wouldn't want to hurt someone because we know how bad it would feel. Both attributes enable us to connect with others, facilitate communication at many levels, and, importantly, build trust and comfort in relationships.

Yet popular culture and technology appear to be undermining the development of these fundamental relationship builders in children. As I described earlier, there has been a dramatic rise in narcissism (the antithesis of selflessness) and a decline in empathy among young people in the past two decades. Although we can't assign a cause-effect relationship with absolute certainty, both shifts have come with the emergence of new technology and the extended reach it has afforded popular culture. It isn't difficult to identify some of the specific culprits.

The "it's all about me" zeitgeist of popular culture clearly interferes with the development of both selflessness and empathy. Children see indifference and callousness play out in many forms of media daily, and research has found that media that depict violence desensitize children to it. Whether reality TV, hip-hop music, movies, or video games, popular culture encourages the elevation of self above others and, at best, benign neglect and, at worst, wanton disregard for others.

These persistent messages, with few counterbalancing messages, explicitly condone such antirelationship thinking and behavior. Children have a hard enough time learning empathy without being actively pushed away from it. For example, one study found that children naturally have difficulty recognizing others' emotions. Another study reported that, after playing a violent video game, young people were slower at identifying facial expressions. It may be that viewing violent content made the children view people as less than human or desensitized them to emotional cues. So, the deck is already stacked against children easily learning empathy, and free and unguided exposure to popular culture just exacerbates the problem.

The many hours children spend with technology also discourage the development of selflessness and empathy. The messages from popular culture that I just described are conveyed predominantly through technology. When children are immersed in technology for so many hours, it prevents them from seeing acts of selflessness and empathy and healthier depictions of relationships. It also precludes children from interacting face-to-face with others and practicing selflessness and empathy. So children are faced with a triple whammy when it comes to learning how to develop positive relationships. First, they're bombarded with messages that teach them to be narcissistic and uncaring. Second, they have inadequate exposure to messages that convey selflessness and empathy, which might otherwise counteract the influence of popular culture and technology. Third, time spent immersed in popular culture and technology is time not spent experiencing selflessness and empathy as both the giver and the receiver.

Family Relationships

Nowhere is popular culture and technology's impact on children's relationships more noticeable than in families. Both influences have contributed to a growing divide between how children perceive their parents and the way parents really are. For example, over the past two decades, children who watch television have received messages from popular culture telling them that parents are selfish, immature, incompetent, and generally clueless from shows like *Malcolm in the Middle*, *Home Improvement*, *Family Guy*, *Two and a Half Men*, and *I Hate My Teenage Daughter*, not to mention reality TV shows such as *Supernanny* and the *Real Housewives* franchise.

This divide has grown in several ways as a result of the increased use of technology among children. First, children's absorption in technology, from multitasking to playing video games, does, by its very nature, limit their availability to communicate with their parents. One study found that when the working parent arrived home after work, his or her children were so immersed in technology that the parent was greeted only 30 percent of the time and was totally ignored 50 percent of the time. Another study reported that family time was not affected when technology was used for school but did hurt family communications when used for social reasons, because children were so immersed in social media that they didn't spend as much time communicating with their parents. Interestingly, children who spent considerable time on a popular social networking site indicated that they felt less supported by their parents.

Second, as digital immigrants, research has shown that parents can struggle to gain proficiency and comfort with the new technology that their digital-native children have already mastered. This divergence in competence in such an important area of children's lives makes it more difficult for parents to assume the role of teacher and guide in their children's use of technology. Thus, many parents lack the authority, at least in the eyes of their children, to regulate its use, and children become unwilling to listen to their parents' attempts to guide or limit their use of technology. Because of parents' anxiety or apprehension about the use of technology, they may be unwilling to assert themselves in their children's technological lives.

Third, computer and mobile technology have allowed children to independently communicate with their friends and others. Consider this: in previous generations, if children wanted to be in touch with their friends, they had to call them on the home phone, which might be answered by a parent. Thus, parents had the opportunity to monitor and act as gatekeepers for their children's social lives.

Times have changed. With mobile phones, instant messaging, and social networking sites, new technology offers children independence from their parents' involvement in their social lives. Of course, children see this technological divide between themselves and their parents as freedom from their parents becoming overinvolved or intruding in their lives. Parents, in turn, see it as a loss of connection to their children and an inability to reasonably oversee their safety and overall health. At the same time, perhaps a bit cynically, children's time-consuming immersion in technology may also mean that parents don't have to bother with entertaining their children, thus leaving them more time for themselves.

There is little doubt that technology is affecting family relationships on a day-to-day level. Children are instant messaging constantly, checking their social media, listening to music, visiting their favorite websites, playing video games, and watching television and movies. Because of the emergence of mobile technology, these practices are no longer limited to the home; children can stay connected in cars, at restaurants—in fact, anywhere there's a mobile phone signal.

It's not only the children who are responsible for the growing divide between parents and their offspring. Parents can be equally guilty of contributing to the distance that appears to be increasing in families. They are often wrapped up in talking on their mobile phones, checking email, or watching TV when they could be talking to, playing with, or generally connecting with their children.

Interestingly, parents have attempted to counteract this growing divide by joining their children in cyberspace. A phenomenon that has caused considerable debate involves parents "friending" their children on Facebook (about 50 percent do so). Some parents use Facebook to keep track of their children's coming and goings. Other parents friend their children as a means of feeling closer to them. So what is their children's reaction to being "friends" with their parents? I did an informal survey with dozens of teenagers and found that the dominant reaction can best be characterized as "Eeewww!" Most children don't want their parents to be their "friends" (or their friends, for that matter).

The fact is that family life has changed in the past generation. The size of homes has grown by 50 percent. Family members can retreat to their own corners of the house, so there's less chance that parents and children will see one another (and this distancing also makes it more difficult for parents to monitor their children's activities). Because everyone is so busy with work, school, and extracurricular activities—not to mention all the time that everyone spends online—there's less time for families to spend together. If we're not careful, it could get to the point at which parents and children are emailing and texting one another more than they're talking—even when they're at home together!

The ramifications of this division are profound. Less connection—the real kind—means that families aren't able to build relationships as strong as they could be, nor are they able to maintain them as well. As a result, children will feel less familiarity, comfort, trust, security, and—most important—love from their parents. There is also less sharing, so parents know less about what is going on in their children's lives and, consequently, have less ability to exert influence over their children. Parents also have difficulty offering appropriate supervision and guidance, and, at a more basic level, they are less able to model healthy behavior, share positive values, and send positive messages to their children.

Friendships

As your children develop and enter the social world outside of your home, their peers will become more important to them. In fact, as your children progress through high school, their peer group will exert a sometimes dismayingly great influence over them as you feel your own relationship with them diminish. Basically, being liked and having friends becomes a central part of their self-identity. That pursuit of friendship has been dramatically altered by new technology.

At one level, social networking has been a boon to offline friendships. Friends can stay in regular contact and share ideas, feelings, and experiences in real time without the barriers of distance or time that used to limit them. In addition, social media affords children the opportunity to practice communication skills, gain confidence in social interactions, and develop friendships with the greater comfort that comes with mediated relationships.

Social networking also lets children express themselves in different ways and gauge the reactions of others. There is some evidence that the more time young people spend on social media, the better they're able to express virtual empathy, which means that they're able to express concern for others through text messages and social media posts. So, in some ways, online technology has extended the meaning and range of friendships in a positive direction.

Yet children's immersion in technology is also having a profound negative impact on how children view friendships. When you look at how technology has changed the definition and meaning of friendships to children, you'll notice several things that place online friendships in a different sphere than face-to-face friendships. Whereas in the physical world the word *friend* is a noun and a condition ("a friend"), in cyberspace it's a verb and an action ("to friend"). The development of conventional friendships is an incremental process that involves deepening stages of shared communication, trust, and openness. Online, friends are made in the click of a mouse, unilaterally, and with little or no communication between the "friends." Old-school friendships are private; online friendships are decidedly public.

Among other differences, there is one noticeably stark distinction between traditional and online friendships: in real life, children focus on the quality of their relationships, but online, children care about the quantity of relationships. In real life, the goal is to have a few really good friends. With social media, the goal—which is obviously in the best interests of the social networking sites—is to accumulate as many so-called friends as possible. Children who use social media frequently get the message that quantity trumps quality; children may come to value friendships in terms of numbers rather than depth.

"Defriending"

Technology has also created another term in the lexicon of friendships: *defriending*. Friendships often dissolve in real life, but it's not always difficult. Sometimes, friendships fade away with time and absence of contact, so the impact on children tends to be minimal. Other times, there is a conflict that precipitates the end of a friendship. In this case, although there may be ill feelings, the breakup is private, there are clear reasons for it, and both children had an understanding and perhaps some control over what happened. In contrast, the so-called defriending that occurs through social media can be more painful than losing friends in the real world because it's usually abrupt (a click of a mouse), unexplained, and sometimes public. Defriending through social media can also be crueler because of the distance and disconnect that technology provides during a conflict. Children tend to be nicer when face-to-face, because they see the impact of their rejection on their friend, and thankfully, most children don't like to hurt others. Do you remember the line from the 1979 film *Alien*? "In space, no one can hear you scream." Well, in today's connected world, that could be modified: "In cyberspace, no one can hear you scream."

With this constant exposure to the false messages from popular culture and technology about what friendships are, a concern is whether those messages will begin to shape how children approach, create, and maintain relationships offline. And, of course, all that time spent accumulating online friendships is time not spent nurturing face-to-face friendships and practicing healthy relationship skills.

What the Research Says

Because the widespread use of technology is a fairly new phenomenon—dating back only about ten years—researchers are playing catch-up as they attempt to study its impact on our lives. Although scientific exploration of the use of technology is growing daily, there is still a dearth of rigorous understanding of the influence of technology on children's lives. The research that exists is decidedly mixed in its praise and condemnation of the role of technology in the lives of children.

Some research has indicated that technology isn't harming relationships. For example, one survey found that almost 50 percent of Twitter and Facebook users indicated that they were spending more time with their friends offline than before they began using the social networking sites. Another survey indicated that respondents felt that while social media helped them to be more connected with family and friends, they preferred to spend time with family and friends in person. Another survey found that teenagers who use online communication felt closer to their offline friends. And an extensive survey by the Pew Foundation reported that the number of people who report feeling socially isolated, a perceived danger of excessive use of technology, hasn't change appreciably in the past twenty-five years. Moreover, technology use is associated with more extensive and diverse social ties, greater community involvement, and spending more time in public places.

Other research, however, has offered a less glowing representation of the role technology plays in children's social lives. Teenagers in one study reported that they didn't feel as close with friends when they were instant messaging them as they did when they connected with them in friends or in person. They also found instant messaging less enjoyable. Other research found that social media was used as a tool for validation of the self (e.g., through enhanced online personae and the accumulation of friends) rather than for building and maintaining relationships. Still another study found that increased video game and Internet use was related to more risky behaviors (e.g., alcohol and drug use, more sexual activity) and poorer relationships. Yet other research showed that active Facebook users engaged in more antisocial and aggressive behavior.

Then I came across what might be the most unsettling finding of a recent survey: whereas previous generations—baby boomers (birth years 1946–1964), generation X (1965–1979), and even the net generation (1980–1989)—indicated that they preferred to communicate face-to-face, the so-called iGeneration (1990–1999) reported that texting was their first choice for communication, followed by instant messaging, Facebook, and telephone in second place, and face-to-face coming in a distant third. Obviously, this finding is simply a reflection of the times—and technologies—in which different generations are raised. At the same time, this shift in preferences may have serious implications on the ability of this and future generations to establish real-life relationships.

I want to emphasize that, because the studies are correlational in nature, all the research, whether supportive or critical of technology use, can't make conclusive statements about whether social media actually causes the problems described here. This means that there is no way to assign a cause-effect relationship between the use of technology and the positive or negative outcomes reported in the research. So there is no way to judge, for example, whether increased video game and Internet use causes risky behavior or whether those young people who engage in risky behavior are more likely to play video games and surf the Internet.

Relationships and Kids 3.0

I hope that I've convinced you that technology can have great benefits in forming and maintaining a variety of relationships. At the same time, if technology is not used with limits and parental guidance, it may prevent children from developing the essential relationship qualities and skills that have allowed us to make real connections and build real relationships for ages. There is certainly a place for children to have online relationships, but they are no substitute for the depth and breadth of flesh-and-blood relationships that allow your children to fully connect with—see, hear, smell, touch, sense, and feel—other people and to completely experience the meaning, satisfaction, and joy of deep human relationships.

Yes, children's (and adults') real relationships can be untidy, with hurt feelings, anger, frustration, and disappointment. They're like two sides of the same coin; children can't experience the beauty of relationships—love, comfort, and excitement—without also being willing to accept occasional blood, sweat, and tears. I challenge anyone to show me that online relationships can provide that.

To raise Kids 3.0, you must first recognize that popular culture offers few healthy messages about relationships to children. At the same time, online relationships may offer some benefits (along with some risks). So, you must help your children strike a balance so they learn to ignore the messages about relationships from popular culture and use technology as a tool to build new and strengthen existing healthy relationships online.

A Word of Caution

A word of caution about the value of educating your children about relationships in this way: if your children are exposed to popular culture and technology at an early age, they may not be mature enough for you to talk to them about those messages. When they're young, your children are sponges that soak up any outside messages that are compelling and persistent. In addition, the influences that popular culture and technology have on children are subtle and often unconscious, so they may not be sophisticated enough to parse out the messages that are usually hidden behind entertaining images, characters, and narratives. Consequently, they may not be old enough to filter the messages from popular culture and technology or to benefit from your attempts to educate them about the messages. Even your best efforts to inform them and their best efforts to make good choices about relationships probably won't be sufficient to prevent many of the messages from getting through and influencing them.

You must recognize that you won't always be able to control what aspects of popular culture your children experience once they're old enough for school and other activities outside their home. Moreover, as digital natives, your children will, regardless of what you believe or want, have a significant presence in cyberspace. As a consequence, as I have noted before, you can't just play defense against popular culture and technology. To raise Kids 3.0, teaching your children about healthy relationships may be your most important strategy in helping them resist the unhealthy messages from popular culture and technology, and in ensuring that they are capable of developing healthy relationships.

Set Limits

Of course, the most basic way to prevent popular culture and technology from having an undue and unhealthy influence over your children's relationships is to set limits on their exposure to the former and their engagement in the latter. You should establish clear expectations about the quality of the popular culture that your children are allowed to experience and the type and quantity of technology they are permitted to use. Just as important, you must create appropriate consequences to add bite to the expectations you set to discourage your children from transgressing from the rules.

A word of caution: if you limit your children's time with popular culture and technology, you may be leaving them with considerable time on their hands, particularly if they're accustomed to unfettered use. So, it's your responsibility to help them find interesting and meaningful alternatives to fill their time with. Otherwise, they will probably not only be bored and feel the urge to test your resolve; they will have plenty of time to feel and express their anger and resentment at the limits you've placed on them. So, for example, you can plan outdoor time or art projects that will not only give your children a healthy replacement for their involvement with popular culture and technology but also send healthy messages about relationships and strengthen your own relationship with them to boot.

Educate

Another obvious preventive measure is to educate your children about the messages they're getting from popular culture and technology. The more informed your children are about those messages, the less vulnerable they will be to them. As they get older, your children will be able to make deliberate choices about what aspects of popular culture they expose themselves to and what technology they use. Part of this education can involve talking to your children about the unrealistic messages that popular culture conveys to them about relationships, for example, that love can be found in a matter of weeks or that physical appearance is a healthy foundation for relationships. You can also show them the differences between online and offline relationships, particularly what is missing from the former and present in the latter, such as facial expressions, body language and other nonverbal cues (notwithstanding Skype and other video chatting), voice inflection (notwithstanding phone calls), touch, and smell.

Model Healthy Relationships

A good place to start teaching your children about healthy relationships is with your relationship with your spouse. Let me say this clearly: there is no greater influence on how your children come to see relationships than your relationship with your other half. From a very early age, your relationship—good, bad, or ugly—becomes the template that their future relationships are based on. If, through your daily relationship with your spouse, you can show your children how a healthy relationship works, you will instill in them a positive view of relationships that will be resistant to those that they receive from popular culture. Also, when you model the healthy use of technology as a tool for strengthening relationships, for example, staying in touch with your spouse by telephone, text, or Skype when away, you provide your children with another template that will encourage the dominance of offline relationships, teach them how to use technology to foster healthy relationships, and make them less vulnerable to the allure of online relationships.

Give Them Social Experiences

The most powerful way to override the inevitable messages about relationships that your children will receive from popular culture and technology is to give them many real-life social experiences. These experiences can help them build the competence, confidence, and comfort to develop healthy relationships throughout their lives. These encounters can include the spectrum of relationships, including family, friends, educational, athletic, cultural, and spiritual. This depth and breadth of flesh-and-blood relationships will also give your children the ability to compare and contrast those relationships and online relationships. Hopefully, they'll see that the latter can't hold a candle to the former. The more ways in which your children can experience the richness of offline relationships, the more they will come to value them and not value those gained through popular culture and technology.

In addition to maximizing your children's in-the-moment appreciation for face-to-face relationships, you can also actively teach them essential relationship skills. Early exposure to social skills and the basics of relationships—such as saying hello and good-bye and please and thank you, shaking hands, and looking others in the eye—will prevent your children from avoiding real relationships because of doubt, shyness, or social discomfort. They'll gain the competence and confidence to explore further unmediated relationships. When you combine direct experience in relationships with the tools needed to build self-assurance in your children's relationship capabilities, they will be in a position to see for themselves that real-life relationships are far more rewarding than those found online.

Raising Kids 3.0: Relationships

- List the ways that popular culture and technology interfere with your children developing healthy relationships.

- How have popular culture and technology changed your relationship with your children?

- What can you do to ensure that your children develop healthy relationships with family, friends, and others?

Chapter 9

Health: Use It or Lose It?

"I was itching, like a crackhead, because I could not use my phone."

—American college student

L et me state this up front and unequivocally: popular culture offers little benefit to your children's health and can cause your children significant harm. The messages popular culture sends to your children about their psychological and emotional well-being are in no way aimed to ensure their positive development; instead, they're aimed to manipulate them to create more profit for its purveyors. Messages from popular culture about self-identity, happiness, immediate gratification, and narcissism, just to name a few, only hurt your children's mental health.

Popular culture and technology don't do your children any favors physically either. Between food advertising directed at children and the sedentary lifestyle that popular culture and technology encourage, healthful eating, regular exercise, and quality sleep—the three most essential contributors to physical health—easily go by the wayside.

A Word of Caution

Again, I want to reiterate that the research I discuss in this section doesn't establish a cause-effect relationship between exposure to popular culture

and technology and these physical, psychological, and emotional problems. At the same time, whether they are causes or effects (it's most likely
a combination of the two), this steadily growing body of research has
painted an overriding picture that unfettered and unguided access to
popular culture and technology does considerably more harm than good
to children's health.

Physical Health

Your children's physical health is the foundation for everything they
become and do. As corporeal beings, they, like the rest of humanity, are
at the mercy of the fitness of their bodies to handle the ordinary challenges
and extraordinary demands that are placed on them during childhood and
beyond. You are responsible for ensuring that your children treat their
bodies well so that they continue to function properly for their lifetimes.
This means getting sufficient sleep, a balanced diet, and regular exercise.
Unfortunately, the world your children are growing up in is not only not
helping you accomplish this goal; it's actually doing everything it can to
interfere with your efforts.

Lack of Exercise

As I noted earlier, children now spend, on average, more than seven and
a half hours a day interacting with technology. That doesn't even include
screen time devoted to school! What do you think children did with
that substantial amount of time before this new technology came along?
Before the advent of electricity, children most likely worked a lot and
played a little, primarily outdoors. Then, with the invention of television,
children began spending more time inside, in front of the boob tube. But
with few entertainment alternatives, children by default went outside and
engaged in physical activity—they ran around, played tag or kick the can,

climbed the monkey bars, or rode their bikes. Plus, schools provided daily physical education classes that contributed further to their fitness.

Unfortunately, research has shown that many of today's parents are afraid to let their children play outside unsupervised, thus forcing children to entertain themselves indoors, where physical activity is limited. Additionally, gym classes are few or nonexistent in schools today as a result of misguided priorities and budgetary cuts.

Technology also contributes to this harmful physical influence on your children. Instead of going outside to play or exercise, many children stay indoors and surf the Internet, engage in social media, or play video games (OK, Wii provides some exercise but, according to research, isn't comparable to real physical activity). The result? One-third of American children are overweight or obese, and 70 percent of them will become obese adults.

The essential question to ask is, what role do popular culture and technology play in what many consider a public health crisis? A growing body of evidence suggests that they play a significant role. For example, one study found that, among children and preteens, increased daily media use was associated with poorer physical health. For preteens, daily video-game playing was also a predictor. For teens, daily video-game playing and daily hours online were also related to poor health. Importantly, this research controlled for demographics (e.g., age, ethnicity) and eating and exercise habits, thus strengthening the argument that popular culture and technology alone were significant contributors to poor health among young people.

Junk Food

The torrent of advertising directed at children and teenagers comprises primarily fast food, sugary cereal, candy, and highly processed snack-food advertisements (72 percent of all ads aimed at them, in fact). Strategies for marketing unhealthy food to children using so-called old media, notably television and radio, include repetition (repeating the same commercial during Saturday-morning cartoons), branded characters (Chester the Cheetah, Cap'n Crunch), catchy slogans ("They're great!"), product placement (ET eating Reese's Pieces), merchandising tie-ins (SpongeBob Squarepants or Shrek dolls and toys), and giveaways (Cracker Jack: "A prize in every box").This junk food is a significant contributor to the epidemic of obesity that has consumed (pun intended) our country. Research has demonstrated that the more time that children spend in front of a screen, the more they ask for unhealthy food and drinks, and—because of what the researchers call the nag factor—parents often give in and give their children junk food.

The emergence of social media has created cross-promotional opportunities that have only strengthened this influence. The advent of new media in the past decade has allowed popular culture to create supersystems that include websites (Candystand, sponsored by Kraft), YouTube videos, Facebook pages, Twitter feeds, video games, tracking software and spyware, online and video games, and viral and stealth marketing—all of which expose children to even more undue influence on their eating habits.

High-Risk Behavior

The influence of popular culture and technology may also extend to unhealthy and potentially dangerous habits. One study reported that teens who use Facebook and other social media have significantly higher rates of tobacco, alcohol, and marijuana use, and they are more likely to have sex at an earlier age. The researchers suggest that widespread and persistent exposure to images depicting these behaviors make them more acceptable and may cause teenagers to feel left out if they don't engage in them.

For example, teenagers who watched more than two hours of television daily were 35 percent more likely to have sex than those who watched less television. Interestingly, when these high users had parents who strongly disapproved of their having sex, the risk rose to 70 percent. When those parents didn't monitor their children's television watching, the risk of sexual activity rose to a whopping 250 percent. However, it should be noted that this study was able to establish a connection only between television watching and sexual behavior—it wasn't able to prove that seeing images from popular culture actually causes this increase in high-risk behavior among young people.

Mental Health

In the earlier chapters of part 2, I described to you in great detail the influence that popular culture and technology have on children's self-identity, values, thinking, and relationships. So, it probably doesn't come as a surprise that they also have a significant impact on more specific psychological and emotional aspects of your children's health and well-being, and overall, this influence is more harmful than beneficial.

An analysis of fifteen studies found that increased media exposure, including exposure to television, movies, video games, and the Internet, was associated with violent behavior and isolation. It reported that children who watched violent shows were not only more likely to be more aggressive; they were also more likely to have fewer friends and to be more secluded socially. The researchers concluded that children who are aggressive will have fewer friends and be more likely to be bullies (because they are more aggressive) or victims of bullying (because they are isolated).

Another study of adolescent girls found that the more they used texting, instant messaging, and other social media to discuss their problems—particularly romantic difficulties—the more depressive symptoms they presented. The researchers argued that technology, which enables children to easily and frequently communicate, allows them to "co-ruminate," that is, to dwell on their problems without providing any solutions.

Case Study in Point

To give you a sense of the scope of the effect of popular culture and technology on the psychological and emotional health of young people, I'll describe the results of a recent international study involving more than one thousand students from ten countries across five continents. This study asked students to disconnect from technology for twenty-four hours. I think you'll agree that the results and insights are startling, disturbing, sobering, and just a little bit hopeful. To give you a preview of the findings, the nouns most frequently associated with this period of disconnection were *addiction*, *failure*, *boredom*, *confusion*, *distress*, *loneliness*, *anxiety*, and *depression*—not one feel-good descriptor in the lot. The study revealed the overwhelming and inseparable role that technology plays in young people's lives.

Not surprisingly—given the students' seemingly unhealthy relationship with popular culture and technology—a clear majority was unable to last twenty-four hours unplugged. A Chilean student screamed, "I didn't use my mobile phone all night. It was a difficult day…a horrible day. After this, I CAN'T LIVE WITHOUT MEDIA!" As with many aspects of our popular culture, young people (and many adults, for that matter) seem to have lost sight of what *need* means. People may really, really, really want their smartphone, MP3 player, or tablet, but *need* should be associated with more elemental requirements such as food, water, and shelter.

Technology seems to be shifting from a tool that people use to, as the study suggests, something that is a part of who we are, an element of our identity and sense of self—almost as if we are becoming cyborgs without the implantation. When separated from their technology, many students described themselves as feeling lost, incomplete, confused. A student from Lebanon said, "The idea of my phone kept jumping into my mind. I was not eager to message or call anyone[;] I was more eager to just 'see' my phone in front of me."

Abstention from media revealed an unrecognized loneliness among the students who participated in the study. They realized not only how shallow their relationships were when mediated by technology but also that their deepest relationship was with their technology. "All I wanted to do was pick up my phone and become a part of the human race again," said a U.K.-based student, without realizing the irony in his statement.

The study also showed how reliant young people were on their technology for stimulation and the degree of boredom they experienced without it to amuse them. Their dependence on technology was illustrated by their lack of initiative and imagination to find their own ways—devoid of technology—to entertain themselves. Said another Chilean college student, "I started to think about things to do without media, and found out that actually I couldn't think of many."

Just so I don't end this section on such a downer, there was a small ray of optimism that came out of this research. Many participants said that the twenty-four hours of disconnection were an eye-opener and wake-up call. Many were shocked to learn how much time they actually devoted to popular culture and technology. They also noticed how the quality and depth of their relationships improved while unplugged. Wrote a Mexican student, "I interacted with my parents more than the usual. I fully heard what they said to me without being distracted."

Others learned that they could actually enjoy life without the leash of technology. Said a U.S. student, "I've lived with the same people for three years now, they're my best friends, and I think that this is one of the best days we've spent together. I was able to really see them, without any distractions, and we were able to revert to simple pleasures." The one-day vacation from cyberspace also put the use of technology in perspective. Another student from Mexico observed insightfully, "Media put us close to the people who are far away but they separate us from the ones who are nearby."

On a further positive note, about 25 percent of the sample actually saw the benefits of unplugging. A number of students learned that they didn't really *need* technology and could survive without it. In fact, some students experienced a transcendental moment in which, for that one disconnected day, they walked the path of quiet and calm and saw that there was much to be gained from unplugging from technology and plugging into life. Said another U.S. college student, "I became more aware with my own thoughts. I realized that maybe it's important to disconnect every once in a while and let your brain remember you."

Internet Addiction

Addiction was the most widely used descriptor of the one-day moratorium on technology in the research I just described. Internet addiction is commonly characterized as excessive use of the Internet that interferes with daily functioning and that can lead to distress or harm. There is considerable debate within the mental health field about whether dependence on technology is a true addiction, like alcohol, drugs, or sex. In fact, the American Psychiatric Association, which produces the *Diagnostic and Statistical Manual* (think shrinks' bible), decided not to include Internet addiction in the latest revision. Some experts in the field argue that the unhealthy dependence on technology may be a symptom of some more fundamental pathology, such as depression or anxiety, and that so-called Internet addicts use technology to self-medicate and relieve their symptoms.

In support of this view, a review of research from the past decade has found that adolescents who demonstrated Internet addiction scored higher for obsessive-compulsive behavior, depression, generalized and social anxiety, attention-deficit/hyperactivity disorder, introversion, and other maladaptive behaviors. This research also revealed an interesting pattern of parental involvement: those youths who were judged to have an Internet addiction said that their parents were lacking in love and nurturance and were overinvested, unresponsive, angry, and severe disciplinarians.

Despite this uncertainty in the psychological community, the students in the survey made it clear that they believe Internet addiction is very real. It certainly passes the duck test (if it looks like a duck and sounds like a duck, it's probably a duck). Not only did the students miss the functions that the technology offered, like texting, surfing the Web, and listening to music, but they actually craved the devices themselves. Said an English student, "Media is my drug; without it I was lost. I am an addict. How could I survive 24 hours without it?" Added an American student, "After experiencing this dreadful 24 hours, I realized that our obsession with media is almost scary. I could not even begin to imagine the world if it was media-free."

Facebook Depression

There's no doubt that Facebook is one of the most powerful forms of media for communication today. More than 800 million users chat, share photos, and regularly keep their friends up to date on their lives. Yet along with other forms of social media, there is a dark side to its use, which has been called Facebook depression, in which children experience symptoms of depression and feelings of not measuring up when they compare their social media metrics, for example, their accumulation of "friends," photos, and status messages, to their peers. But don't let the name fool you—this phenomenon also includes anxiety, other psychiatric disorders, and a range of unhealthy behaviors.

Perhaps the most comprehensive study to date found that Facebook overuse among teens was significantly correlated with narcissism. Among young adults, Facebook overuse was also associated with histrionic personality disorder, antisocial personality disorder, and bipolar disorder, as well as sadistic, passive-aggressive, borderline, paranoid, and somatoform personality disorders. The study also explored the strength of Facebook use as a predictor of these psychiatric disorders and found that, even when demographics such as age, gender, median income, ethnicity, and education were controlled, Facebook use was one of the three strongest predictors.

The Attraction of the Internet

So what do people gain from Internet use, and how does its use become an unhealthy behavior often associated with addiction? One study examined the types of gratification that people gain from the Internet. It found that four specific forms of gratification were cumulatively the best predictors of Internet addiction: virtual community (feeling connected to a group), monetary compensation (money they earned through various web-based activities), diversion (distraction from their lives), and personal status (the feeling of individual standing they gained from Internet use). These types of gratification are normal for children, yet there is something about the Internet that morphs them into unhealthy needs that appear to become addicting.

This so-called addiction appears to go deeper than just psychological dependence. There is emerging evidence indicating that our interaction with technology produces the same neurochemical reaction—a burst of dopamine—as that from alcohol, drugs, sex, and gambling addictions. Persistent exposure to technology-related cues, such as the vibration from a smartphone announcing the arrival of a new text message or the ping of an incoming tweet, can cause people to get caught in a vicious cycle of dopamine stimulation and deprivation. Moreover, the brevity of technology, such as 140-character text messages, lends itself to this vicious cycle because the information received isn't completely satisfying, so people are driven to seek out more information for their next shot of dopamine. Imagine your children growing up with this relationship with technology and the strength of its grip on them if they are allowed ungoverned and unguided use of technology.

There's Good, Too

Certainly, the research I've just described doesn't paint a very rosy picture of popular culture and technology's influence on children. The findings aren't all bad though. Studies have shown that children who spend more time with social media show increased virtual empathy (i.e., empathy expressed through technology) and real-world empathy (which is considered a separate but related factor). The best predictor of virtual empathy was the time spent on Facebook and the use of instant messaging. More of both forms of empathy means that children are receiving more social support, which is always a good thing for children.

Social media can also, as I've noted previously, help those young people who experience shyness or social anxiety. Research has found that introverted young people can gain comfort and confidence in social interactions in several ways. Shy children can use social media to overcome what is perhaps their most difficult challenge, initiating new relationships, in a low-risk environment. They can avoid awkwardness that is endemic to making friends by allowing themselves to gain familiarity with others and build friendships online. Introverted children can also practice social skills with the relative distance and safety that social media afford.

One study indicated that popular culture and technology can actually improve family relationships and encourage feelings of connectedness. It noted three emerging trends. First, popular culture and technology can be used as a point of entry into children's lives and can create opportunities for sharing. Second, they enable families to have quality time and pursue activities of shared interest. Third, popular culture and technology can be used to teach children essential life lessons, thereby enhancing socialization and increasing children's awareness of sensitive issues.

Another study reported that social media have educational benefits for children. Children are learning practical skills that are necessary for success in today's technological world. Specifically, children are learning how to use and become proficient with technology, developing their creative abilities, appreciating new and different perspectives, and enhancing their communication skills.

Yet another study indicated that prosocial video games, ones that promote compassion, cooperation, and other healthy values (e.g., Zoo Vet, Animal Crossing), encourage helping behavior. The researchers found that young people were more likely to help others after playing a prosocial video game as compared to a neutral one. In a related study, researchers observed a similar effect when children were given the opportunity to protect a stranger who was being harassed.

There is some research suggesting that children use technology to better cope with stress in their lives. Technology can potentially mitigate stress in a number of ways. First, technology provides children with more outlets to express their feelings of stress, thus allowing for a cathartic effect. Second, one of the most robust findings related to managing stress is that social support can act as a buffer against stressors. Technology, including Facebook postings and instant messaging, enables children to receive more, immediate, and diverse support from a wider range of people. Third, technology can allow children to find useful information that may help them to reduce their stress. Finally, technology may act as a distraction and a means of distancing children from the stressors, thus providing a respite from the stress and giving them the time and perspective to deal with the stress more effectively.

You may have noticed that I described research that offered some contradictory findings; for example, popular culture and technology prevent and foster empathy. For parents, this lack of consistency is frustrating because it's difficult to draw firm conclusions and make informed decisions about the role of popular culture and technology in our children's lives. These studies certainly highlight the complexity of this relationship and the need for further exploration. In the meantime, all we as parents can do is educate ourselves about the available research as best we can and use our best judgment in deciding the kind of relationship we want our children to have with popular culture and technology.

Kids 3.0 and Health

Balance is the operative word in raising Kids 3.0, who are both physically and mentally healthy. By *balance*, I don't mean that you should balance the healthy with the unhealthy. In that scenario, the unhealthy (popular culture and, to a certain extent, technology) would have far too great an influence on your children, and that effect would be largely harmful to them.

A nutritional analogy works well here. You first need to make sure that your children get the proper nutrition they need in their lives by offering them a psychological, emotional, intellectual, social, physical, and spiritual diet that will fuel their vigorous development, in addition to fostering healthy self-identity, values, thinking, relationships, and life (as detailed in part 2). Once this nourishment is in place and helping your children grow strong mentally and physically, you can then introduce other foods, namely popular culture. Like sweets, popular culture may not be healthy, but your children should be allowed to indulge in it periodically in reasonable portions because it brings your children pleasure. Technology is a bit different from popular culture because it does have nutritional value for your children. Many aspects of technology, whether searching the Internet for information or maintaining relationships through social media, can be healthy for your children in their own right. Plus, your children need to learn these skills to successfully navigate the digital world they'll live in. At the same time, too much of a good thing or using technology past the point that it nourishes your children will obviously do them harm.

Kids 3.0 and Physical Health

As I have mentioned, you can't just play defense in your efforts to ensure that popular culture and technology don't interfere with your children's healthy development. Instead, you need to proactively create opportunities that will encourage your children's physical health in spite of popular culture and technology. You should also recognize that, in your efforts to ensure their physical health, you aren't just fulfilling their immediate physical requirements for a healthy childhood. Just as important, you're setting your children on a road of healthful living, helping them develop healthy defaults for years to come. There are three main areas of your children's physical health you should focus on: eating, exercise, and sleep.

Eating

You need to make certain that your children are getting a balanced diet that meets their nutritional needs for their particular stage of physical development. That may seem like a no-brainer, yet the robustness of the junk-food industry and the current epidemic of childhood obesity would suggest that many parents aren't feeding their children the right foods in the right quantities.

Although a detailed discussion of healthy nutrition for children is beyond the scope of this book (there are numerous books, newsletters, and websites devoted to healthy eating), you can approach your children's diets in the same way you approach their intake of popular culture and technology. In other words, you want to create a balanced diet. But a balanced diet doesn't mean you would feed them half healthy foods (e.g., lean meats, fruits, vegetables) and half junk food (e.g., fried food, candy, soda). Such a ratio would likely put your children on the road to a life of obesity and ill health.

Instead, ensure that their diets are predominantly healthy, say 80–90 percent, and that the remaining 10–20 percent of less nutritious foods would be for their enjoyment and not enough to hurt them. Let's be honest here: children love treats—whether cake, ice cream, candy, or salty snacks. Although these usually offer little to no nutritional value to your children, in small quantities these foods will realistically do them little harm, yet they will offer them immense pleasure. My gosh, could you imagine a childhood without treats? Importantly, though, for your children to grow up healthy, you must limit their intake of treats and guide them in making healthy choices among the universe of unhealthy foods that are readily available to them and that popular culture is pushing on them.

How healthful your children's diets are depends on three things. First, what you eat. It's simple: if you eat junk, your children will eat junk. If you eat well, so will they. Second, and related, is what you have in the house. If your fridge and cabinets are filled with junk, that's what your children will eat. If you have predominantly healthy foods, that's what your children will eat. Third is what you feed them at meals. If you put unhealthy food in front of them at meals—well, you get the picture.

If you start your children eating well from the start, then they'll ingrain those defaults, and healthy eating will become a habit and a lifestyle. If, however, after years of unhealthy eating you've decided to change their diets well into childhood, you will probably get some pushback. In this case, you'll want to make this shift gradually rather than cold turkey by slowly increasing the healthy foods available to them and slowly decreasing the unhealthy foods that they can eat. You should do your best to make those healthful foods as tasty as possible so your children can learn that food doesn't have to be bad to taste good. Of course, you can still give them treats—just don't make them a dominant part of their diets. More than anything, you must be persistent in the face of what will probably be considerable and loud resistance. I have learned that if children are hungry enough, they will eat anything. As part of this nutritional retraining, you will also want to educate them about healthy eating, because when they walk out your front door, they will be entering an environment quite hostile to good nutrition, from cafeteria lunches and what your children's friends are eating to the food messages on billboards and other advertisements.

Exercise

Unfortunately, popular culture and technology are not friends to physical exercise. Aside from Wii, Kinect, and other systems that aim to re-create sport and exercise virtually (and that, as the research indicates, are inadequate substitutes for actual exercise), most of what popular culture and technology offer children acts to prevent them from being active and engaging in exercise. Media—for example, watching television or movies, surfing the Internet, using social networking, or playing video or online games—encourage your children to sit down and be sedentary.

As I have argued throughout this book, the first step is to limit your children's use of popular culture and technology. If they can't, for example, watch television or play video games, then they have to do something else. If they can't figure out what to do with the free time they have once you've established limits, then you can help them find something to do. You can sign them up for sports lessons or leagues or have them take dance classes. Or, here's a real mindblower: make them go outside and play!

Your children are also more likely to value exercise if you are active yourself. When your children see you enjoying yourself while exercising or hear you describing how good you feel after working out, they'll naturally want to feel the same way. You can also include them in your physical activities by having them participate in running, biking, swimming, soccer, skiing, or other sports.

Sleep

Sleep may be the most important, though overlooked, contributor to your children's physical health. The reality is that children can survive without exercise and on little healthy food, but all children need sleep. It's often unnoticed because you don't usually see your children sleeping, and the benefits of sleep are not readily apparent (though the costs of not sleeping usually are).

Yet the influence of sleep on children is profound. Quality sleep has been found to be associated with improved attention, reduced stress, greater emotional control, better mood, improved memory, greater ability to learn and retain information, better grades, lower risk of obesity and other health problems, and a longer life.

Sleep experts say that children ages three to six need thirteen hours of sleep, seven- to twelve-year-olds should get eleven hours, and children ages twelve to eighteen need nine hours of sleep each night. Disturbingly, research has shown that children are staying up later and not getting enough sleep these days. One study confirmed the value of "early to bed, early to rise": children who went to bed early and awoke early got more exercise and were healthier and thinner. In contrast, children who went to bed late and woke up late were more likely to watch television, use computers, play video games, and snack on unhealthy foods during those late evening hours. Plus, they were more likely to view advertising for unhealthy food. As a result, these children engaged in sedentary activities more often than physical activities. Not surprising, these children were more overweight than children who had better sleep habits.

The question is, why are this generation's children not getting enough sleep? It is not surprising that technology is one culprit. According to several surveys, upward of 70 percent of children have televisions in their bedrooms. A television's presence in children's bedrooms translates into more hours watching; according to one study, children with televisions in their bedrooms watched about 50 percent more than those without televisions in their bedrooms. Television viewing is, not surprisingly, significantly related to lack of sleep.

With the explosion of technology in the past decade, computers and access to the Internet have become significant causes of late nights and lack of sleep (more than one-third of children have computers and Internet access in their bedrooms). Children are spending a substantial amount of time surfing the Web, interacting with friends on social media, instant messaging, and playing online games when they should be sleeping.

An increasing amount of homework is also keeping children up at night. Homework has increased by 50 percent in the past three decades, and much of that increase comes from more homework being assigned to early elementary school students. This has occurred despite considerable research that homework has only limited benefits to academic performance, particularly for younger students.

When you have tired children with too much homework, you also have an increase in the use of stimulants, such as caffeine, to keep them awake. In fact, one study reported that 75 percent of children consume caffeine daily. The ready availability of caffeinated sodas, the cultural acceptance and popularity of children drinking coffee, and the popularity of energy drinks have created recent generations of caffeine junkies, a default that is likely to continue into adulthood. The unfortunate side effect of these caffeinated kids is late nights awake and long days exhausted.

Given the obvious benefits of a good night's sleep and the clear harm caused by not enough sleep, it's your responsibility to ensure that your children develop good sleep defaults and get a good night's sleep. The great thing about sleep is that there are a lot of practical steps you can take to help your children get more sleep.

Start by recognizing the importance of quality sleep and making it a priority in your family and the default for your children. If sleep is important to you (and it should be: you'll experience similar benefits and consequences to getting quality sleep or a lack of sleep, respectively), sleep will be important to your children. At a practical level, establish quality sleep habits for your children. These sleep practices include removing televisions and computers from your children's bedrooms and creating end-of-evening quiet time and consistent bedtime routines. Of course, you can't really control the amount of homework your children receive, but you can do your best to ensure that they devote sufficient time to it earlier in the day and evening. This means not allowing them to be distracted by popular culture and technology so their homework doesn't keep them awake late at night. The added benefits to these quality sleep practices is that your children won't feel the need to amp themselves up with stimulants to stay awake, they'll do better in school, and they'll just plain feel better during the day.

Kids 3.0 and Mental Health

You can approach your children's mental health in much the same way that you approach their physical health. All your efforts will help you to help your children develop a healthy relationship with popular culture and technology, to make good decisions about how they interact with them, and, ultimately, to learn to use popular culture and technology in ways that minimize the harm and maximize the benefits for their mental health.

These preventive steps will partially mitigate the harm that popular culture and technology can do to your children's mental health. But, as with physical health, you can't only play defense when it comes to ensuring such an essential contributor to your children's development and well-being. Instead, you need to consider what you can do proactively to lay the foundation for your children's mental health. If you take these steps, you can be confident that your children will have the psychological, emotional, and interpersonal capabilities to have a healthy childhood and lead a successful and happy life in adulthood.

It just so happens that everything that I address in *Raising Generation Tech* is devoted to accomplishing the fundamental goal of ensuring your children's mental health. The topics that I explore in part 2, namely self-identity, values, thinking, relationships, health, and life, are the very foundation of their mental health. That robust mental health is synonymous with raising Kids 3.0.

> ## Raising Kids 3.0: Health
>
> - Identify the physically and mentally healthy and unhealthy messages your children get from popular culture and technology.
>
> - Do your children exhibit any symptoms of Internet addiction?
>
> - How can you be a role model for your children's physical and mental health?
>
> - What steps can you take to ensure that your children eat well, exercise regularly, and get a good night's sleep?

Chapter 10

Life: What's It All Mean?

"It's weird when you have to text your kids [in your house] to come to the dinner table."

—*Susan, mother of three*

Beyond the specific areas you should prepare your children for to live in this crazy new world of technology and popular culture, there is an overriding way you can best ready your children for what lies ahead: you need to prepare them for life. You must ensure that your children see life as it really is, not as it is presented to them by popular culture or through the lenses of technology. Only by doing so can you ensure that your children develop a perspective about the unmediated world that is accurate and that will allow them to thrive in it.

Unfortunately, popular culture presents children with a false mirror through which they view life; it doesn't give them a true characterization of what real life is. For example, so-called reality TV holds no resemblance to real life. Cable and local news, which live by the axiom, "if it bleeds, it leads" and thrive on sensationalism, offer you a distorted view of danger in your children's lives. Technology offers your children an incomplete depiction of life because it restricts what can be experienced and offers limited options from which to choose.

With too much exposure to popular culture and excessive use of technology, your children may develop a disconnect between how they perceive life and the way life actually is. For example, because of the popularity of reality TV shows, which millions of children watch, and the ease of becoming a "celebrity" on YouTube, the perceived distance of fame grows closer and seemingly more attainable. In fact, as I noted previously, research has shown that children today indicate that wealth and celebrity are their top life goals.

Reality TV shows such as *Jersey Shore* (the most watched show among young teens) send the message to children that anyone can become famous and rich with little talent or effort. At the other end of the "life" continuum, reality TV shows like *Teen Mom* and *16 and Pregnant* glamorize teen pregnancy and make young parenthood look easy.

Without a realistic representation, your children will develop a "bizarro" view of life and, as a result, will act on the world not as it is but rather as popular culture and technology have shown it to be, however erroneous that may be. The result? Your children will be left unprepared for real life.

Virtual versus Real Life

To help clarify what I'm talking about, let's first look at some fundamental differences between life as depicted by popular culture and the life that exists for most children in the real world. Popular culture depicts life as being dominated by wealth, materialism, celebrity, status, and physical appearance. Real life for most people has none of those attributes, and the chances of children attaining, for example, wealth or celebrity are very small.

Life, as conveyed by popular culture that spotlights, for example, movie and television stars, professional athletes, and celebutantes communicates to children that an easy life, immediate gratification, and entitlement are rights, and success with little effort is the rule rather than the exception. Real life, in contrast, can be difficult: rewards are often years away, and people don't always get what they deserve. In addition, accomplishments are gained only through hard work and perseverance, and, even then, there are no guarantees. Yet for children who have unrestricted and unguided exposure to popular culture, its depiction of life is the life that they come to believe exists. These children are in for a rude awakening when confronted by a life that, for most of us, bears little resemblance to the life media portrays.

Now let's consider the differences between life as experienced through the lens of technology and so-called real life, which happens away from technology. First, digital life is, by definition, virtual, which means any experience created by technology with the aim of replicating actual experience. The problem with online reality is that, although it shares similarities to real life, it is missing important elements. For example, email exchanges can be a wonderful means of communication, but they lack visual input (so important to effective communication), the nuance of facial expressions and body language, and clear emotional content. In contrast, real life is, well, real in its fullest meaning of the word, that is to say, meaningful, relevant, and complete.

Second, mediated life is limited by the technology that makes it possible. There is always something between your children and their experiences—a text message isn't the same as conversing with a friend directly, and a Wii sports game doesn't have the benefits of participating in the actual sport. As I just noted, a great deal is missed in this mediated experience. Conversely, real life is unmediated, which means that children experience life directly and immediately with all the accompanying benefits and messiness, both of which are essential for your children to learn how to navigate life.

Susan Greenfield, the British neuroscientist whom I introduced in chapter 4, has articulated some compelling concerns related to the mediated nature of technology. She believes that, although new technology appears to offer freedom, it is actually a largely closed system that comprises a series of options that children are forced to choose from. In contrast, she advocates for a free-range world in which there are no limits set on the choices that children have. Greenfield suggests that the fixed quality of technology may inhibit the development of creativity, which is, by its very nature, open and undefined. Relatedly, she argues that the emergence of linguistic and visual imagination will also be hindered because of the limited and prescribed opportunities that are presented with technology. Moreover, children have little reason, incentive, or need to be creative when linguistic and visual images are supplied to them. Greenfield is also critical of the "contracted, brutalised" writing skills inherent in Twitter and text messages that lack the vocabulary and structure essential for sophisticated thinking and expression.

Greenfield believes that many forms of technology, including video games and Facebook, place too great an emphasis on process and the satisfaction of goals without consideration of context and personal relevance. For example, in video games, action is often without values, meaning, or consequences. Yet it is that narrative and individual significance that provide children with the moral framework to place experiences in a realistic and meaningful context.

At an even deeper level, Greenfield concludes that, because children's brains are so malleable, the substantial changes in the world they are growing up in will not only affect their thinking and behavior; there will also be, as emerging research is demonstrating, significant alterations in the neurochemistry and structure of children's brains. She cites as an example how dopamine, the influential neurochemical that seems to be significantly affected by technology, has the effect of reducing activity in the prefrontal cortex, the area, as mentioned several times already, most associated with executive functioning including attention, self-control, abstract thinking, planning, and decision making—all attributes that are essential for healthy development in children. Making matters more challenging, the late development of executive functioning makes it easy to see why anything that interferes with its healthy growth could have substantial and generally negative ramifications for children.

At a more visceral level, online life lacks the complexity and, well, untidiness of real life. It seems too safe, too clean, too controllable. There is the anonymity of blog comments, the false intimacy of online relationships, the ease with which you can hit "Delete" or "Exit" whenever it's convenient. Digital life enables children to keep real life at arm's length; for example, teenagers can break up with their boyfriends or girlfriends with a text message or a Facebook posting. Without the immersion in real life, they miss out on the richness of what life has to offer—its joys and thrills and its trials and tribulations.

Real life, by contrast, is inherently complicated and messy. Children have only so much control over their sensations, emotions, thoughts, behaviors, and experiences. Real life is undefined, unstructured, and unrestricted. There is frustration, sadness, anger, and fear. There is also excitement, contentment, and love. Real life encompasses the fullest and richest of experiences, unfiltered and uncensored. When you ensure that your children experience this unmediated life, you allow them to learn and practice the skills necessary to navigate that sometimes chaotic life. Without those skills, children will be unprepared for real life as they progress through childhood and into adulthood.

As a parent, you think about real life, and your first reaction may very well be that you want to protect your children from such disorder and potential hurt. Giving them ready and unrestricted access to popular culture and technology is one way to safeguard them from real life, you might think. Yet to do so would be to act in your own best interests—you hate to see your kids struggle and feel bad! But I'm sure that, when you're able to step back from life just a bit, you'll see that sheltering your children from real experiences would be a disservice to them. When you allow your children to absorb themselves fully in real life and guide them through its many ups and downs, you fill their development with texture and depth that simply can't be replicated in the online world.

Wired but Disconnected

The next time you're walking down the street, at the gym, in an elevator, out for a run, or even at your local coffee shop, look at the mostly young people around you and note what you see. What I notice is the ubiquity of people with headphones or earbuds with wires snaking down to their laptop computers, MP3 players, and mobile phones. These wired people are definitely growing in number as more digital natives reach a certain age. Admittedly, wired music is really not new technology, with the Sony Walkman dating back to 1979, but the size, capacity, and low cost of music players and the proliferation of multiuse devices like smartphones has made it more available and practical for frequent and widespread use.

The result of this convergence of technology is that many children spend much of their waking day existing in a no-man's-land in which they are surrounded by life but not connected to or immersed in it. The ongoing stimulation generated by earbuds restricts other senses, such as sight, by drawing children's attention away from the outside world in general (just like talking on a mobile phone while driving). You might think that earbuds would enable children to spend quality time inside their own heads, but, paradoxically, although they are blocked out from the external world, they also pull their attention away from their internal world, thus keeping children in a state of mind that is neither here nor there, not connected to either the internal or outside world.

The question that I keep coming back to is, why the need to be constantly tuned in (to whatever children are listening to) and tuned out (of the world around them)?

My discussions with many children indicate that they wear earbuds constantly for a variety of reasons. At a basic level, children wear them because, when they look around, they see that this is what digital natives do; teenagers and young adults listen to music with earbuds, so it's natural that younger children want to emulate them.

Also, anyone who has walked down a sidewalk in New York City or another big city knows the overwhelming cacophony of sounds that assaults them. Children may find this sensory overload in their external world aversive, and earbuds reduce the auditory onslaught. Of course, this doesn't explain the omnipresence of earbuds in the suburbs and rural America, and on college campuses.

More insidious, being digital natives who are always connected with technology, children have become dependent on it for stimulation. Because they've been connected from a very early age and their parents may have encouraged them to use technology to entertain and placate them, this generation of children may have never gained the ability to be bored, to just be alone and unstimulated with themselves, or have learned how to keep themselves occupied without being tethered to technology.

Children may use music to block out the maelstrom of thoughts and emotions that constitute their internal worlds. Using earbuds can distract them from unpleasant aspects of their lives and away from the angst that can crowd their minds. Music can act as makeshift self-medication, artificially generating positive emotions, whether excitement (e.g., heavy metal), contentment (e.g., classical), or inspiration (e.g., theme from *Rocky*), or even "misery loves company" emotions, such as anger (hip-hop) and melancholy (country).

Earbuds can also allow children to avoid engagement with others. Whether because of a sense of inadequacy, social discomfort, or fear of rejection, when children wear earbuds, they ensure that they don't have to interact with others and can be confident that others won't try to connect with them.

When children cut themselves off from themselves and those around them, several unhealthy things may happen. First, without the ongoing experience of children's own thoughts and emotions, the self-awareness and self-control that are born from spending time inside of one's own head aren't allowed to develop. Children simply don't get to know themselves and, in this absence, are unable to fully gain confidence in who they are or mastery over their inner lives. Without this experience and the accompanying sense of who they are, children may be more vulnerable to external influences on the formation of their self-identity (as I discussed in chapter 5).

Children also don't allow themselves the opportunity to experience and gain competence at relationships. The simple fact is that when children are wired, they're incapable of interacting with others. As I noted in chapter 8, the ability to develop and maintain relationships is a skill that can emerge only with practice. As a result, children may grow up insufficiently skilled and unprepared to have healthy relationships in adulthood.

These consequences may conspire to prevent your children from developing the very qualities you want them to depart childhood with, namely, a strong sense of self, social comfort, and the ability to build and sustain nurturing relationships. All these qualities are essential ingredients for happiness, yet they may be inhibited by the constant distractions from noise between the ears delivered by earbuds.

What Children Miss

Think of all that children miss when they disconnect from both their internal and external worlds. There are those ordinary moments of just being with oneself and the common experience of sensations, thoughts, and emotions that are part of being human. There are also those transcendental moments of inspiration, insight, and creativity that may not arise or may get lost in the crowd of earbud-transmitted sound.

Children also fail to notice much of the beauty (e.g., birds chirping), mundanity (e.g., lawnmower humming), and even ugliness (e.g., cries of help) in the world because, when wearing earbuds, they are in a sensory and psychic limbo that precludes them taking notice of the life that is passing by them. They may also miss out on those less-common, truly awe-inspiring connections with the physical world, such as sunsets, hummingbirds, and the smell of lilacs.

What about those magical connections that are made because of a serendipitous meeting or someone taking note of and reaching out to another? They would be missed because children don't notice them, and because others are unwilling to break through the earbud-imposed wall of silence and solitude. That person sitting next to or walking by your children could be their future friend, spouse, or business partner. Think of all of the people you have met over the years because you were tuned into life. Consider all those opportunities that your children may miss because they are tuned into the sounds emanating from their earbuds and tuned out of life. At a basic level, the web of human connectivity that binds all of us is largely lost without the ability to communicate spontaneously and directly.

Finally, don't forget about those opportunity costs that I've mentioned previously. The time that your children devote to popular culture and technology—on average, seven and a half hours a day for children age eight to eighteen—is time not devoted to life. When you add up that time, that's quite a substantial chunk of time during which your children are missing out on both important life lessons and great experiences.

I'm not saying that you should confiscate your children's earbuds and prohibit them from ever placing said items in their ears. Music (what the vast majority of children listen to when wired) is a wonderful form of entertainment and can enrich your children's lives. At the same time, when those earbuds become a dominant form of stimulation for your children and an ever-present sentinel of connection with the world around them, I would say that it's time to take pause.

iPhone Syndrome

Being a parent is tough these days. You may be working full-time or just feel like you are because of the time you devote to your children and all the far-too-many activities they're involved in. It seems like just about every moment of your day is scheduled, leaving no time for yourself. You feel like you're on a runaway train, trapped, stressed, overwhelmed, and just hanging on for dear life. It's at these moments (or should I say hours?) when you're vulnerable to one of the most dangerous aspects of parenting: expediency.

Expediency occurs when family life overcomes you and you resort to doing what is easiest for you, not what is best for your children. Unfortunately, parental expediency and what is in the best interests of children don't usually play well together. Instantly pacifying children when they're cranky, for example, may be the path of least resistance for you in the short run, but it is not the best path for your children's development in the long run, and it will definitely not help you raise Kids 3.0.

Parents have done the expedient thing with their children to make being a parent easier for as long as humans have roamed the earth. Back when we had just become *Homo sapiens*, cave parents gave their cave kids a stick or bone to keep them occupied. As our species has evolved, so has the sophistication of parents' strategies for acting expediently. Toys became increasingly mind absorbing, and with the discovery of electricity, a new era of parent expediency emerged. Dolls could walk and talk. Toys moved, played sounds, and lit up. The radio helped, although without visual stimulation it just couldn't hold children's attention for very long.

Then along came the real game-changing tool in parents' expediency toolbox. Yes, folks, the television. Television gave parents an infallible method for keeping their children entertained for hours by flipping a switch (or later, pressing a button on the remote). Believe it or not, even now, the television continues to reign supreme as parents' first tool of choice for expediency with their children. The television had its limits though; it worked only at home. By the turn of the new millennium, parents had a new and growing toolbox (or should I say "arsenal") of electronic gadgetry to make raising their children easier.

The march of technology is inexorable and the creative genius that has spurred this era of technological innovation stepped up to the plate and provided parents with increasingly sophisticated ways to pacify their children. Of course, there was the computer, video-game consoles, and DVD players that kept children occupied at home. The call of the wild outside of the house beckoned, and technology heard the call.

First came portable video-game devices followed by the portable DVD player, which enabled parents to be expedient in restaurants, on airplanes, and in cars. Even that wasn't enough to make parents' lives easier. Automobile manufacturers got into the act, providing built-in DVD, video-game, and music players and screens in cars, minivans, and sport-utility vehicles, thus making those long (or short) car rides a breeze for parents and children alike. Thanks to popular culture and the latest technology, you now have more ways than ever to keep your kids distracted, entertained, and otherwise occupied—in other words, out of your hair.

All these technological advancements have resulted in the pièce de résistance of parental expediency—the iPhone and its army of clever app developers—and the emergence of what I call iPhone syndrome. The iPhone is truly the Swiss Army knife of parental expediency, offering children video games, music, movies, and even drawing in one small and portable package. (I'm sorry to pick on the iPhone when there are many similar smartphones in use. I've seen children who are attracted to iPhones like a heat-seeking missile but show no interest in other smartphones, even when they look virtually identical.) Now, no matter where you are—in a car, in the woods, at a park, during a family gathering—your children can be entertained or quieted by that small yet hypnotic screen.

Don't get me wrong. There is a place for expediency; it's necessary for parents to maintain their sanity in the often-overwhelming world of raising children in the twenty-first century. Parents have the right to some time of their own to do grown-up things such as talk to another adult, bathe, or have a martini.

My concern is when twenty-first-century expediency becomes the default mode for raising children. Instead of talking to or playing with their children or helping them find something to do on their own that might allay their frustration, boredom, or whining, parents just pull out their iPhone and hand it to their children.

What are the ramifications of children who aren't left to their own devices (no pun intended) when they don't have anything to do? Just about everything that interferes with children becoming Kids 3.0. First, recent research suggests that excessive use of technology triggers the same neural pleasure-inducing activity in the brain as do drugs, sex, and gambling (as discussed in chapter 9), and from what I've seen, this finding holds true for children whose parents give them unfettered access to their iPhones (and iPads, for that matter).

The inability to be bored may also have serious implications later in life. Let's face it, many jobs, in the factory, store, or office, are boring. If this new generation was weaned on the iPhone to entertain them, where do you think they'll turn when they get bored at work (and how do you think that will affect their job performance and productivity)?

Technology-dependent children may also lose their initiative. When parents immediately give children their iPhones when they become bored, cranky, or bothersome, children are deprived of the opportunity to figure out how they might get out of their stimulus-deprived doldrums on their own. As I'm sure you can see, lack of initiative will present real problems in adulthood.

Patience, or the ability to delay gratification, is one of the most significant predictors of positive behaviors in adolescence, including higher grades, less alcohol and drug use, and less sexual activity. Yet the immediate gratification of parents giving their iPhones to their children to appease them may interfere with their learning to put off rewards until a later time.

Last, children who are immediately entertained may have a harder time developing respect for others. Children may not learn that other people's time is valuable and that parents have other responsibilities beyond their children. Children may fail to realize that respecting others can mean sitting and waiting patiently until their parents finish what they're doing.

I'm not trying to demonize iPhones; they just happen to be the most ubiquitous and egregious example of parental expediency in our technological landscape. Nor am I suggesting that parents who use their iPhones periodically to assuage their children are going to scar them for life. At the same time, I would argue that parents who use their iPhones as the default means of occupying their children are, at best, doing a disservice to them, and at worst, they may be doing some real harm to their long-term development.

Keep in mind that the iPhone syndrome is only a specific example of the overall misuse of technology in raising children. The iPhone could be substituted with any form of technology or media, and the impact would be the same. The bottom line is that, as I have emphasized throughout *Raising Generation Tech*, you have to be conscious of technology's influence on your children and make sometimes-difficult decisions about that use that is in their best long-term interests.

Kids 3.0 and Life

To raise Kids 3.0, you must ensure that both popular culture and technology assume an appropriate and in no way central or influential role in your children's lives. Only with this approach can you be sure that your children develop an attitude toward life that is both healthy and grounded in the reality of life that exists for most of us.

There may be no more powerful epiphany for you than that your children's experiences in their formative years will largely determine how they perceive, define, and engage in life for the rest of their lives. That may cause you to say, "Oh my gosh!" because of the significant ramifications of that realization. You may feel as if your children engage with popular culture and use technology appropriately and responsibly and are on a good path for understanding what life is. If so, then I say, "Bravo!" Or you may feel trepidation as you have come to realize as you read this book that popular culture and technology have been playing too great a role in defining life for your children. If the latter, don't beat yourself up with recriminations for what you might have done, and definitely don't despair. Instead, take this epiphany as a call to action. It's never too early or too late to help your children define or redefine what life means to them.

So, the question you are probably asking now is, how do I make certain that my children learn about life as it really is rather than by how popular culture and technology tell them it is?

As I have emphasized throughout *Raising Generation Tech*, the first basic step is to limit your children's exposure to popular culture and immersion in technology. The simple reality is that the less time that your children are involved with popular culture and technology, the less influence they will have on them. At the same time, you can't just outlaw their exposure entirely; that wouldn't be fair to your children because it would prevent them from enjoying the many aspects of both. You also don't want your children to resent you for not allowing them to do what most all of their peers are doing. You must, then, strike a balance to allow some involvement with popular culture and technology, but not so much as to be harmful.

The second basic step is to be well informed about popular culture and technology and to use that knowledge to educate and guide your children into making healthy decisions on their own about their use. As your children develop, you will have increasingly less influence and control over their choices because much of their lives will be occurring outside of your home. When you provide that balance and the knowledge and tools to decide for themselves how much and what popular culture and technology they wish to engage in, you help ensure that they make good choices and prioritize life over all else.

Part of setting limits involves establishing expectations and consequences about your children's interaction with popular culture and technology. This process often involves "forcing" children to do things that they don't like but that you deem important. You should expect that your children spend much of their day disconnected from popular culture and technology and connected with life. Given the omnipresence of both in digital natives' lives, your children may not like it and will let you know in no uncertain terms. You should realize that even their grumbling and grousing, though quite unpleasant, at least allows them to experience life. In this case, life's disagreeable moments offer them opportunities to deal with their attitude and emotions related to your decision and their relationship with others, most notably, you.

You should also practice what you preach by curbing your own exposure to popular culture and technology and making certain that you make life your priority. Look at your involvement with popular culture and technology and assess whether you are being a good role model for your children. Do you devote undue time to, say, reality TV shows? Are you constantly checking your smartphone for emails and text messages or surfing the Web without a specific purpose? As the saying goes, "actions speak louder than words," and that adage is no less relevant for sending messages to your children about the relationship that you and your children have with popular culture and technology and life.

You can also make life a priority for your family as a whole. You can, for example, institute no-tech and no-pop-culture days in which your family has a moratorium on unnecessary popular culture and technology. These days can be devoted to sharing fun and interesting experiences that are neither mediated nor distracted by popular culture and technology. When you and your family connect to life together, you not only ensure that your children experience life fully but also strengthen your relationships, which, as I'm sure you know, is an essential part of having a fulfilling life.

I encourage you to protect your children from popular culture and technology and anything else, for that matter, that you deem potentially harmful. At the same time, I encourage you not to protect them from life itself which, though sometimes hurtful, is rarely truly harmful. In other words, don't overprotect your children. It's natural for you to be scared for your children's safety and want to protect them from life's bumps and bruises. But when you don't allow your children to fall down and go boom, literally and metaphorically, you prevent them from experiencing life's normal ups and downs. You also preclude them from learning essential life lessons that can only be gained when they are allowed to experience life fully and unmediated by parental involvement.

Yes, life is sometimes difficult and messy and unkind. As a parent, you feel your children's pain, and it hurts you too. What your children need often is to be left to their own devices when faced with life's challenges (with you standing at the ready in case they really need you). With freedom from overprotection, you give them the opportunity to find solutions to life's problems, gain life skills, and build resilience, thus preparing them for life outside your home and away from your guidance. What is the alternative? You keep them in a cocoon of unreality in which you ensure their immediate safety while leaving them ill equipped for the life that lies ahead of them.

Raising Kids 3.0: Life

- How accurate are your children's perceptions about real life?

- How much are your children wired but disconnected from life?

- What symptoms of iPhone syndrome do you see in your children?

- What can you do to be less expedient with your children?

- What can you do to better ground your children in real life?

Part III

The Hard Work and the Payoff

Chapter 11

Do the Job You Signed Up For

"[My daughter] just went nuts...She slammed doors. She accused us of being overly conservative when all of her friends are able to do things at night. She didn't speak to me for three days. She broke things. You're left with the choice of do I make her a leper because she's not a part of this or do I just spend all of my time fighting?"

—Beverly, after she prevented her daughter from texting between
9 p.m. and 6 a.m. on school nights

*R*aising Generation Tech is predicated on the idea that popular culture and technology may be the most powerful forces in your children's lives, influencing them psychologically, emotionally, and socially; overtly and subtly; and positively and negatively. Moreover, popular culture and technology are inherently neither good nor bad, but, at the same time, they are not neutral. Popular culture and technology become potentially harmful when your children have unguided and unlimited access and exposure to them. But when you can filter the healthy from the unhealthy, your children can use popular culture and technology to their benefit.

On the basis of what you've read so far in this book, I don't expect that you're going to throw out your television, computer, mobile phones, and video consoles, or every one of your children's toys, games, and pieces of clothing that may send an unhealthy message to them, or all of the food and drink in your kitchen that offers no nutritional value. Nor should you. Doing so would deny your children the many benefits that both popular culture and technology have to offer. Moreover, such draconian efforts wouldn't prevent them from being exposed to popular culture and technology anyway. And such actions would certainly not endear your children to you!

At the same time, I'm quite sure that you want to do whatever you can to protect and prepare your children for the crazy new world of popular culture and technology. Despite the frequent feelings of frustration and despair that are just part of being a parent, you do have the power to both protect and prepare them. In fact, research shows that what kind of parent you are is related to your children's Internet behavior. Specifically, authoritative parents, who are characterized by warmth, nurturance, and give-and-take—but also appropriate limits, expectations, and consequences—have been found to be associated with more knowledge, involvement, and supervision of children's use of the Internet. Not surprisingly, their children have more positive online behaviors, lower rates of Internet addiction, higher self-esteem, and lower incidences of depression than children whose parents were authoritarian (i.e., strict, unloving, and punitive), indulgent (i.e., permissive, overly involved, and few expectations), or neglectful (i.e., disengaged, emotionally unsupportive, undemanding).

Being an authoritative parent means taking charge of your children's popular cultural and technological lives, making deliberate choices about the role that they play in their lives, and taking active steps to shape their engagement with popular culture and technology. In addition to the recommendations I have offered to this point in *Raising Generation Tech*, there is more you can do to protect and prepare your children for this crazy new world.

Your Relationship with Popular Culture and Technology

The greatest impact you have on your children's relationship with popular culture and technology is your relationship with popular culture and technology. Recognize that your children learn so much about their world early in their lives not just by what you tell them but, more powerfully, by seeing what you do in your world. The values and attitudes that you hold and the involvement you have with popular culture and technology will, more than anything, dictate how they relate to these two forces.

If you devote considerable time to, for example, watching reality TV, online gaming, and reading celebrity and fashion magazines, your children will come to value and want to do the same. Alternatively, if you eschew all things popular culture and technology, your children will probably develop a similar attitude and express little interest in them. These two examples obviously lie at the extreme ends of the popular culture and technology continuum, and your relationship with both probably resides somewhere in between the two poles.

As I have discussed earlier, it's important that you realize that your children aren't the only ones vulnerable to the messages conveyed by popular culture; you're susceptible too. Gosh, you're also human and, as such, can be seduced by many of the same whistles and bells that popular culture and technology offer, just in grown-up form. You may become absorbed in cooking shows on television, addicted to your email, or prone to surfing the Web when you're bored. As human beings, we also have needs to feel good about ourselves, to be accepted by others, and to feel like we're in the know. Popular culture spends billions of dollars every year figuring out the sirens' calls that will draw you in, because it knows that if it hooks you, it has a very good chance of hooking your children.

In acknowledging the significant influence you have over your children in simply being who you are and doing what you do, your first step in deciding on the relationship that you want your children to have with popular culture and technology is to explore your own relationship with both. Here are some questions you should ask yourself:

- Which aspects of popular culture and technology do you devote your time and attention to?
- What messages do these activities you participate in send to your children?
- Are these messages ones that you want your children to receive?
- Are you willing to change your relationship with popular culture and technology if it's in the best interests of your children?

Only you can answer these questions. Only you can decide whether your relationship with popular culture and technology is a beneficial or harmful influence on your children. And only you can have the power to change your relationship if you deem it necessary.

If you're comfortable with your relationship with popular culture and technology and don't feel that it's sending harmful messages to your children, then you can move to the following section, which discusses how you can more actively shape their relationship with pop culture and technology. However, if, after this analysis, you've come to the conclusion that your relationship with popular culture and technology is not setting a healthy example for your children, you need to make some potentially difficult choices about the messages you're sending your children.

Be Active

What is clear is that the more knowledgeable and involved you are in your children's connected lives, the greater your influence over what they're exposed to and the choices they make, and the better you can ensure that their involvement with popular culture and technology is healthy and balanced. In fact, one study reported several factors that determined how satisfied parents were with how they influenced their children's online behavior and protected them from risk. The parents who felt that they had the greatest influence were well informed about both the technology itself and their children's use of it, and they were more actively involved in their children's digital activities, knowing what they did and how much time they spent doing it. They adopted an authoritative parenting style that emphasizes clear expectations and boundaries while also encouraging dialogue and independence. They also engaged in frequent discussions with their children about their online experiences. The takeaway from this research is that the most informed and engaged parents felt the most effectual in guiding their children's digital lives.

Another study offers four ways in which parents can protect and prepare their children for influences from popular culture and technology:

- Cocooning involves parents shielding their children from unhealthy outside forces by setting clear limits on media use.
- Prearming means that parents give their children the information and skills they need to resist the unhealthy messages themselves.
- Deference refers to parents expressing trust in their children's capabilities to protect themselves by allowing them to use some media without limits or supervision.
- Compromise involves parents balancing restrictions on media use with giving their children some autonomy to make their own choices.

All the strategies that I discuss in this book fit into one of those four categories.

Study Popular Culture and Technology

An essential step in ensuring that your children keep popular culture and technology in perspective is for you to really understand it. That is obviously a challenge for digital immigrants; many parents are just happy to be able to navigate the basics of email, the Internet, and their mobile phones. To immerse yourself in popular culture and technology to the extent needed to understand what your children are experiencing requires a real effort. You need to study the popular culture your children are exposed to and the technology they experience it through: watch what your children watch on television, play their video games, listen to their music, and visit the websites they surf. Get to know Facebook, Club Penguin, YouTube, and other websites they may frequent.

Then, understand the messages your children are getting from popular culture. Yes, there are media that are educational, teach positive values, and are simply entertaining, but they are the exception rather than the rule. The sad reality is that the vast majority of messages that popular culture communicates to your children aren't healthy. For example, television shows, movies, and video games glamorize violence, sexuality, wealth, celebrity, and the use of alcohol, drugs, and cigarettes. Fashion and celebrity magazines affect how girls think about their bodies, the amount they diet and exercise, and the occurrence of eating disorders. The Internet gives your children limitless access to a universe of inappropriate information and people, ranging from pornography to cyberstalking. Instant messaging and texting are not only a pretty significant distraction and waste of time, but, as we frequently learn from the news, a means through which children make tragically bad decisions that hurt themselves and others.

With this knowledge, you're in a position to make deliberate decisions about what popular culture and technology you allow your children to experience. With this information, you gain the power to protect your children from the values and practices that you deem unhealthy and prepare them to use popular culture and technology in a way that benefits them most and prevents them from experiencing the pitfalls.

Deconstruct Popular Culture and Technology

Popular culture, through its many forms of media, is sophisticated in the ways of deception and manipulation. If you just look at the surface of popular culture's messages, they can appear quite benign, filled with, as I discussed earlier, entertaining characters, fun music, and eye-catching images. If you look no deeper, you may conclude that those messages are harmless, but then you leave your children exposed to the potential risks that exist below the surface. Popular culture spends billions of dollars each year finding ways to shape your children's values, thinking, emotions, and decisions, and in doing so, their attitudes, habits, and behaviors, without them (and perhaps you) even realizing it.

An essential step in protecting your children from this influence is to deconstruct popular culture and technology by looking beneath the surface of the fun and entertaining content and the particular medium that is being used to see the real messages that they are sending to your children. A great exercise is to study a social networking site that your children are involved in:

- Recognize what attracts your children to it (e.g., social networking sites offer constant and instantaneous interaction and reinforcement).
- Identify how the social networking sites may be manipulating your children (e.g., exposing them to targeted advertisements and tracking their preferences).
- Recognize the messages that may lie below the surface (e.g., quantity is more important than quality of friends; self-promotion is more important than self-expression).

- Consider how this interaction with technology affects your children (e.g., sedentary, absence of direct face-to-face interaction).
- Compare these messages to those that you want to convey (e.g., depth and substance of relationships, physical activity, direct human contact).
- If the messages from popular culture and technology are incompatible with yours, make a deliberate decision to limit your children's exposure (e.g., limit the amount of time devoted to social media; provide alternatives such as sports, games, or reading).

You can also use this method to study other forms of media your children use, such as television shows or video games.

Be aware that you don't have to openly endorse popular culture and technology's messages for them to influence your children. When you allow your children to play video games, spend significant amounts of time with social media, or eat junk food, you're conveying your tacit approval. Because you typically express displeasure with your children when you don't like something they're doing, when you don't express it, they will assume that what they're doing is OK. The lesson here is that when you ignore your children's unhealthy behaviors, that is as good as encouraging them.

Be a Gatekeeper

Protect your children early in their lives by being their gatekeeper to popular culture and technology. You should not allow this relationship to be dictated by expediency or your children's nagging or tantrums, or by their peers or friends, and definitely not by popular culture. To the contrary, you must consciously and deliberately decide what they watch, play, listen to, surf, communicate with, and use. You must make that decision on the basis of your understanding of the benefits and costs of popular culture and technology combined with the values and attitudes you hold about them.

Your goal is to maintain control over your children's exposure to and use of popular culture and technology early in their lives. In doing so, you can protect them from the many bad messages that they communicate. You can also, as I discussed in chapter 3, instill in them healthy defaults on the appropriate exposure to and use of popular culture and technology.

As the gatekeeper, you can educate them about the messages of popular culture and the uses and misuses of the technology they are surrounded with. You can also get them away from popular culture and technology altogether by encouraging them to spend their time doing other things, such as reading, participating in sports, or playing a musical instrument.

Establish Limits

As the gatekeeper, establish limits on how much time your children are allowed to spend with technology, and determine what they're allowed to watch, play, listen to, surf, and use. For example, you may decide to prohibit your children from watching more than one hour of television each day (and only after they've finished their homework and fulfilled their household chores), playing video games during the week, or using the telephone or texting during dinner or after 9 p.m.

You ideally want to act as gatekeeper from their very first exposure to popular culture and technology, but you may have decided to make changes after your children have developed unhealthy habits. In this case, if you introduce limits when there were few limits previously, your children may resist your efforts because you've allowed them to establish a less healthy set of defaults. For example, if you previously allowed your children unfettered access to social networking sites and then impose limits on your children's use, they will probably be very unhappy and will likely express their displeasure loudly and in no uncertain terms. In this situation, you may want to gradually wean them off of the social media rather than force them to do it cold turkey. Don't expect them to just stop without providing them with a reasonably compelling alternative; for example, allow them to take up an extracurricular activity that they've wanted to do, in order to engage them and take up the time that they would otherwise be devoting to their social media. Research has also shown that a little bit of bribery can provide a short-term incentive to make a change.

You don't want your children to view you as a dictator who forces prohibitions on them. This approach is a recipe for resistance and rebellion, not to mention a bad relationship with your children. Certainly, at an early age, you have considerable control over your children without any chance of opposition. But as your children mature and begin to assert their independence, you want to bring them into the decision-making process so they feel some sense of ownership and buy-in of the decisions that are made. In general, by age five, your children are old enough to have a conversation with you about the limits you want to set and why you want to set them. When you allow your children's input and demonstrate your willingness to consider their wishes and make compromises, you enlist them as allies in a common cause rather than as adversaries staking out territory.

Regardless of the approach you take, you have to be firm and consistent in establishing limits, expectations, and consequences—follow-through is everything! When parents have followed my advice and thrown out their children's video-game consoles, turned off their televisions, or limited access to social media, they have told me that their children complain— loudly and persistently!—for a while, trying to wear them down. When the parents stuck to their principles, their children, in every case, finally gave up, accepted the change, and found other, healthier ways of entertaining themselves.

Set Expectations for Your Children

You should expect a lot of your children. Set the bar high on what you value, and make it clear to them that you expect them to live up to those standards. Expectations communicate to your children what you, well, expect of them. They are standards of behavior you hold your children to, which are grounded in your family's values, attitudes, and beliefs about who you want your children to become and the life you want your children to lead. Expectations act as guides for your children of what they should and shouldn't do.

Setting expectations for your children is particularly important in their involvement with popular culture and technology. I hope you realize that popular culture communicates its own set of expectations to your children. Of course, these expectations aren't healthy for your children; for example, these expectations include that they should value material goods and that physical appearance and popularity should be important to them. These expectations are based on what is best for popular culture's own bottom line and are in no way connected to the best interests of your children. In turn, technology, by its very nature, sets no expectations; it's the Wild, Wild West of today. You can't expect your children to establish their own expectations in their use of popular culture and technology; remember that the prefrontal cortex isn't fully developed, so you can't count on your children to make reasoned decisions about how they use either.

Although there's a lot of talk about expectations—all parents I speak to agree that they should place expectations on their children—there are powerful cultural forces, not to mention your children's own resistance, that can prevent you from setting reasonable expectations. Plus, parents don't always clearly understand how to set and enforce expectations.

By holding your children to certain expectations, you're implicitly teaching them the values that underlie them. For example, when you establish an expectation that your children will make their homework a priority over their use of social media, you communicate the value of responsibility. They can choose to meet the expectations and reap the benefits (e.g., your approval, good grades, increased responsibility and freedom) or fail to fulfill the expectation and accept the consequences (e.g., your disapproval, poor grades, reduced responsibility and freedom). To maximize the value of expectations on your children, you can do the following:

- Talk to them about the value underlying the expectation and explain why you believe it's important.
- Be specific in the expectations and give them examples of how the expectations apply to relevant aspects of their lives.
- Encourage them to give their input into the expectation and consider modifying the expectation based on their feedback. The more involvement and agreement they have, the greater ownership and compliance they will feel toward the expectation.

Establish Consequences

Establishing reasonable expectations for your children in their relationship with popular culture and technology is essential for protecting and preparing them for the crazy new world they live in. At the same time, expectations without consequences are like a dog with a loud bark but no bite; scary at first, but ultimately harmless. Consequences are what cause your children to initially live up to your expectations. Now, I don't expect you to actually bite your children to get them to behave appropriately, nor does using this metaphor intend to suggest that the consequences you create should hurt your children in any way. Rather, the consequences you connect to your expectations should be just unpleasant enough that, when they're confronted with the option of living up to or failing at your expectations, your children decide that the benefits of doing what you expect outweigh the costs.

It can be difficult for you to have consequences for your children. No parent likes to be the bad cop, and when you establish consequences, you may create conflict and ill feelings between you and your children, which is not something any parent wants. Also, you may establish consequences with the best of intentions, but that little thing called life gets in the way of administering them. It takes time to follow through on consequences when your family life is already overscheduled and harried. It takes energy that you may not always have. Like many kids today, yours may be really good negotiators, possessing the ability to talk you out of administering the full consequence. Promises of better behavior in the future and demonstrations of contrition and love can seduce you into letting your children off the hook (bad idea!).

Having consequences doesn't have to turn you into a Kim Jong-il or a big, green ogre (like Shrek without the sense of humor). Consequences just mean that you're letting your children know that you have some pretty darned reasonable expectations (at least to someone who is not a child) and that they must learn to become a contributing member of your family and our society.

You can actually avoid the dictator or ogre categorizations by including your children in the discussion of expectations and consequences. Clearly state your expectations and establish and communicate the consequences of your children's meeting or not meeting those expectations.

Explain why you're setting the expectations and the consequences so your children can see the benefit of acting in accordance with those expectations, both to avoid the consequences and to learn the lessons embedded in them. This discussion helps ensure clear communication and understanding, and it encourages open dialogue between you and your children, which, by the way, will also reduce the likelihood that your children will play the "you're so much tougher than my friends' parents" card.

Ask your children for input into this process, particularly in coming up with fair consequences. If your children help create the consequences, they'll have a hard time arguing against them when they face your wrath because they failed to meet an expectation. This fairness justifies the punishment to your children when they don't meet the expectations—for example, the Internet will be turned off for the night if they're logged into Facebook when they should be studying. This fairness also encourages them to internalize the expectations because the consequences are not so severe that they feel they're being forced to comply with them (in other words, the punishment should fit the crime).

Consequences must also be meaningful to your children. They need to see the personal value of meeting the expectations. External benefits can include parental approval, improved grades, a later curfew, or receiving some predetermined reward, such as receiving their allowance. Internal value can mean recognizing how the expectations will help them achieve their goals and the intrinsic satisfaction of doing the right thing. If you explain the rationale behind the expectation, create a fair consequence and emphasize that they have the power to choose whether to meet or violate the expectation, then they're more likely to live up to your expectations because they see them to be just and feel ownership of both the expectation and the consequence.

Parents who enforce excessive or arbitrary consequences risk resentment and resistance from their children. If you establish a consequence that your children view as harsh and extreme, for example, taking away their mobile phone for a week if they text during dinner, they may meet the expectation for a while out of fear of punishment but will likely, at some point, rebel against it. Most harmfully, they won't internalize and accept the expectation and the underlying value as their own and will likely cease their efforts to meet the expectation as soon as they are out of your control.

At the same time, consequences that are insufficient for the transgression are equally ineffective. If your children see the consequences as so mild that there is no incentive to meet your expectations, then your consequences won't have, as I noted earlier, enough bite to warrant compliance.

You need to then *firmly and consistently* commit to the expectations and consequences that you establish. If you don't administer the consequence fully and at every opportunity, they will learn the threatened consequences will not always be meted out and, knowing children, they'll probably roll the dice the next time the situation arises. Every time your children are let off the hook without a consequence, the value of the expectation is lost. In other words, your children must learn that you mean business!

Pick Your Battles

Decide which aspects of popular culture and technology you find most unhealthy for your children, and realize that, given the power of popular culture and the omnipresence of technology, you cannot fight and win every battle, especially when your children are outside your home. So pick your battles carefully. Which battles you choose to fight will be based on your own experiences, values, and sensibilities. It may be, for example, that you judge movies that have no commercial merchandising

tie-ins to be OK for your children, but you won't permit them to join
Facebook or other social networking sites until they are thirteen years old
(something many parents allow despite it being illegal; now there's a bad
message to send your kids!). You may decide that you can sometimes live
with explicit music lyrics but draw the line at provocative clothing. You
might even accept an earring for your son or navel ring for your daughter
knowing that children tend to outgrow them.

Whatever you decide, I would encourage you to give your children
some victories in these battles. When you allow your children to win a
few small skirmishes, such as letting them watch a television show that
you deem quite awful or allowing them to text their friends at certain
times of the day, they won't feel the need to seek out bigger wins that
may be more destructive, for example, the use of drugs or alcohol. At the
same time, whichever battles you do decide to fight, commit yourself 100
percent, and don't relent no matter how difficult it gets.

Raise Healthy Skeptics

You can help prepare your children to actively resist the unhealthy aspects
of both popular and technology by raising healthy skeptics. You want
your children to find a healthy middle ground between naïveté (where
they will believe everything) and cynicism (where they won't believe
anything). You want your children to be discerning observers and critical
thinkers who don't accept popular culture's messages at face value or use
technology without a recognition of its potential costs. Healthy skepticism means that they (and you) ask tough questions about those messages:

- Why is the message so attractive?
- What is the real message?
- What does the messenger get out of it?

- Will the message help or hurt me?
- What effect does the technology have on me?
- Do I want to accept this message?

You can foster this healthy skepticism by teaching your children to engage, rather than simply absorb, popular culture and to be active participants in the technology they use. If, for example, there's a social media site that your children like to use—and that you're not thrilled about but decide that the battle isn't worth fighting—you should use the social media with them and explore the answers to the foregoing questions.

This discussion will help your children gain a better understanding of what they're really doing and how it's affecting them. Then, when they're mature enough to act as their own gatekeeper, they can decide for themselves whether to accept the messages. At worst, your children may still engage with certain popular culture and technology because it's fun (and everyone else is doing it), but now, because they're healthy skeptics, they will consciously reject its unhealthy messages. At best, your children will reject popular culture all together by choosing to no longer devote time to it and to use technology only as a useful and balanced tool for communication and education.

Disconnect!

Yes, you heard me right. I said disconnect your family! I realize that is a shocking and perhaps heretical suggestion in a time when many families are connected 24/7. I'm not saying that you have to be thoroughly disconnected; that's not realistic in today's digital world. It does involve limiting your family's engagement with popular culture and technology. It also doesn't mean raising your children to be Luddites. Rather, it means finding times when you can disconnect your family from the matrix.

Consider the many benefits that you and your children would accrue by disconnecting to some degree. Everyone would have more free time that would otherwise be spent in front of a screen. You would spend more quality time with your children, which, in the hectic life you probably lead, both of you would welcome. Your family would be able to have more experiences together that are enriching and just plain fun. The cumulative effect would be closer and stronger relationships with your children and, by extension, a greater ability to positively influence them.

Your children would be less stressed because they would have more time to devote to their studies. They would be more active, which would give them more energy and reduce the likelihood that they would become overweight. Your children would sleep better because they wouldn't be staying up late checking their Facebook pages or playing online games. And they would have more time to actually spend with their friends.

If you have young children, disconnection will be easier if they do not become overly connected in the first place. In other words, from the beginning, raise them in a family environment that is not dominated by popular culture and technology (recognizing that they will be exposed to both outside of your home). This old-school approach means deliberately and actively limiting your children's exposure to either for the first years of their lives (how long is up to you, though the longer the better).

One mother writes about the benefits of raising two children without popular culture and technology: their incredible imaginations, ability to entertain themselves, innocence, and long attention spans. She does say that she will gradually expose her children to popular culture and technology as they get older, for both social and practical reasons.

If your children are already immersed in this crazy new world of popular culture and technology, you could completely disconnect cold turkey. Another mother of three teenagers became frustrated by the lack of real daily connection she had with her children and established a moratorium on all popular culture and technology in their home for six months. No television, no computers, no mobile phones, no video-game consoles, no Internet (although her children were allowed access to screens at friends' houses and at school). She was prepared for an uprising from her children, but, surprisingly, there wasn't one. After a short period of some complaining, her children actually embraced their family's non-tech lifestyle.

Just as surprising, the hiatus from popular culture and technology lived up to this mother's expectations. Her family had meals together frequently, talked more than ever before, and shared many wonderful activities together. Her children were faced with boredom and found ways to overcome it without the crutch of popular culture and technology. They rediscovered things that they had once enjoyed doing, including reading, cooking, and playing a musical instrument. Even after the six-month popular culture and technology vacation ended, their family maintained many of the habits they had developed during the break. The older siblings rarely visit their Facebook pages, the son actually sold his video-game console so he could buy a saxophone, and the youngest continues to study in the library, where social networking isn't allowed.

You could gradually wean your children (and yourself) off of popular culture and technology. You can start with small limits, such as no technology at the dinner table or only an hour of television a day. As you establish these restrictions, you should be ready to offer your children alternative activities so they know what to do with themselves (e.g., talking to one another at the dinner table, playing board games, reading during the previous television time).

As your children become accustomed to the limits that you've set, you can slowly increase those boundaries. For example, you can progress to no television on weeknights or no Internet after nine in the evening.

You can then move to establishing no-tech days, such as on Saturdays. Your goal is to have popular culture and technology (unrelated to work, school, and daily functioning)· be the exception rather than the rule in your family's lives, something that is used but not needed—and, ultimately, something that has no real influence over your children's lives.

Disconnecting may not be easy for your family, depending on the extent to which popular culture and technology are currently present in your lives. Many families these days (both parents and children) are addicted to popular culture and technology. The idea of a family having to entertain itself may seem pretty daunting. It's likely that your children will give you some serious pushback if you've allowed them to become overly immersed in popular culture and technology. At the same time, if you're committed and show your children that you mean business, after a short period of adjustment, I believe that you will find that the benefits that your family gain from disconnecting regularly will far outweigh any costs that you may incur.

Raising Kids 3.0: Your Job

- Evaluate your relationship with popular culture and technology (are you a good role model?).

- Study the popular culture and technology your children are immersed in so you understand the real messages they are getting.

- Be a gatekeeper in determining what popular culture and technology you permit your children to use.

- Set appropriate limits, expectations, and consequences for your children's involvement with popular culture and technology.

- Pick your battles over what popular culture and technology you allow your children to use.

- Raise your children to be healthy skeptics.

- Find times for your family to disconnect from popular culture and technology.

Chapter 12
Meet Your Kids 3.0

"Here are some of the things we love about our [daughter]:
- *[Her] unbelievable imagination*
- *What she does make and do while I'm busy (sometimes that means helping me with chores—it's amazing what little hands can do)*
- *The innocence of her brain and her total lack of sophistication— she has no idea about things like war, sarcasm, or commercials*
- *The malleability of her brain—a rock can still be so many things for her*
- *Her attention span for stories, books, even car rides*
- *Her initiative about playing on her own, and her lack of need to be entertained"*

—Abi, mother of two and parenting blogger

Let's think back to some of the original questions I posed at the beginning of the book: what kind of children do you want to raise? What are the values, attitudes, and skill sets your children will need to thrive in this crazy new world of popular culture and technology? What can you do to ensure that they will walk out your front door ready to thrive in our increasingly complex and unpredictable world?

I'm sure your first instinct is to protect your children from all the ugliness that lies outside your home so that they can enjoy their childhood for as long as possible. But you then might think that such sweet and innocent children would be totally unprepared for the big cruel world that they will be entering; they would be eaten alive by the cold-hearted and voracious beast known as popular culture. Such naive children would be easy prey for all that lurks in every corner of the tech world.

You might feel as if you're caught between a rock and a hard place. You don't want your children to grow up under the sway of unhealthy messages from popular culture and technology. At the same time, you feel compelled to prepare them for that sometimes harsh world that is dominated by popular culture and technology by exposing them to it early and often. You definitely don't want your children to grow up to be shallow, narcissistic, and uncaring. In contrast, your children absolutely must be knowledgeable and skilled in all things digital if they're going be successful in this world that relies more and more on technology both to fulfill our most basic daily functions and to get ahead academically and professionally.

How can you possibly protect and prepare your children for life in this new millennium? Is it possible to raise children who are both unaffected by popular culture and technology and prepared to prosper in a world largely controlled by them?

My answer, as I have shown you in this book, is a resounding yes! You can raise good children with solid values who aren't guileless and gullible little beings. To the contrary, when you make instilling healthy values and attitudes your singular priority, you raise Kids 3.0, that is, children who are better prepared to succeed in this new digital world than those who are raised deeply immersed in popular culture and technology.

Engagement in popular culture and being tech savvy won't necessarily make your children selfish, superficial, and immature. To the contrary, an understanding of what life in the twenty-first century is like is absolutely necessary for raising Kids 3.0. Developmentally appropriate exposure to popular culture and technology can help children gain a healthy perspective that will enable them to come to a nexus of their values and dreams and the seemingly harsh realities of boots-on-the-ground life in the real world. They'll find meaning and fulfillment in a world that isn't particularly interested in helping them find either. The answers to the questions that I've tried to show you in this book are that your children can be both kinds of children, protected and prepared, those that I have labeled Kids 3.0.

What truly exceptional children your Kids 3.0 will be. From their minds to their hearts to their hands, they'll be far more capable than those children raised by parents who don't understand the need to strike a balance between the ideal and real aspects of life in this crazy new world. They'll be far more prepared to meet the cultural and technological challenges that they will face in the coming years while still maintaining their humanity and their soul. So let me introduce you to Kids 3.0.

Mature

The hallmark of Kids 3.0 is their maturity, which I characterize as their ability to act in ways that are both healthy and appropriate in the face of messages from popular culture that promote just the opposite, conveyed through old and new technology. This maturity is expressed in Kids 3.0 who can do what is right even when confronted by pressure from popular culture and peers to do otherwise. An essential part of Kids 3.0 is their ability to let go of immature thinking (e.g., "I'm going to be rich and famous"), emotions (e.g., throwing temper tantrums), and behavior (e.g., needing to be connected constantly) that popular culture and technology encourage.

Popular culture wants your children to stay immature. Immature children expect immediate gratification and depend on others for validation. They are impatient and demanding, and they place their own needs ahead of those of others. They are more easily influenced by outside forces such as popular culture and technology.

Kids 3.0 think (e.g., "How will my action affect others?"), feel (e.g., empathy, compassion), and behave (e.g., help others in need) in ways that attempt to balance self-interest with the interests of others. Mature children can delay gratification, think critically, be self-reliant, resist outside pressure, make thoughtful decisions, and have little investment in popular culture, thus making them immune to its attractions. Mature children are trustworthy, dependable, and thoughtful because they've developed a perspective on life that is grounded in healthy values and a realistic understanding about the way the world works.

Value Driven

Children who are raised to be Kids 3.0 are different from those who have grown up immersed in popular culture and technology without sufficient guidance or limits. Kids 3.0 are guided by healthy and deeply held values (as I discussed in chapter 6), which are becoming progressively lost in our cultural and digital landscape. Essential values, such as integrity, respect, responsibility, compassion, creativity, relationships, justice, tolerance, and independence, just to name a few, act to both protect and prepare Kids 3.0 for life in the twenty-first century. Life-affirming values protect Kids 3.0 from toxic messages by filtering out the negative aspects of popular culture and technology and allowing the positives to pass through. These same values prepare Kids 3.0 for this crazy new world by encouraging the development and use of emerging executive functioning capabilities, such as critical thinking, prioritizing, gaining long-term perspective, appreciating delayed gratification, and having healthy skepticism, that will guide them to make the beneficial decisions and life choices on the basis of what is best for them rather than what popular culture tells them.

Able to Distinguish Need from Want

One of the most fundamental goals of popular culture is to create need where no need exists, for example, the iPhone and *American Idol*. Only by creating voracious need in children can popular culture satisfy its insatiable appetite and fulfill its ever-expanding bottom line. Popular culture exerts this influence on children by causing them to confuse what they want with what they need. It accomplishes this goal by connecting what popular culture wants (which usually involves children buying things) with actual needs that children have, such as the need to feel good about themselves and to be accepted by others.

It's not difficult to see how children who are not getting those real needs fulfilled in any substantial way or who have been manipulated into believing that buying some product would satisfy those needs would be vulnerable to such messages. How often have your children said to you about, say, a video game or iPod, "But Mom, Dad, I need it. If I don't get it, I'll die!"? Last time I checked, food, water, shelter, and love were real needs, and electronics were not. These children are needy and demanding because they have been led to believe that stuff will satisfy deeper psychological and emotional needs.

As a result, popular culture has, in a very real sense, control over children whose parents don't set limits, provide guidance, or offer alternative perspectives and experiences to counter those influences. Popular culture dictates children's perceptions, attitudes, and behavior related to their needs. These manufactured needs end up limiting rather than expanding these children's ability to function in this crazy new world.

Kids 3.0 aren't vulnerable to this exploitation. They see popular culture for what it is, namely a force whose goal it is to control their thoughts and behavior for its own ends. Kids 3.0 recognize the source of the messages and their underlying intention, and they clearly detect their disingenuousness.

Because they have strong and resilient self-esteem, Kids 3.0 aren't vulnerable to popular culture's attempts to manipulate their self-worth. Rather, Kids 3.0 gain self-esteem from real sources, including being loved and respected by others, feeling safe and secure, helping others, and being competent and experiencing success.

They also understand what real needs are and can readily separate those needs from what they want, even when popular culture and peers argue otherwise. As a result, Kids 3.0 are patient, well mannered, and disciplined because they're not driven by a compulsion to have those so-called needs satisfied completely and immediately.

Technology turns wants into needs unintentionally, though no less powerfully, by altering the expectations related to connectivity and stimulation and the neurochemistry involved with it. Think back to when you were young. Your expectation of connectivity was quite low. You could write letters to friends far away, pass notes to friends near by, or call them on the telephone, if you were in your home and willing to stand near a wall or table where the (wired) telephone kept you moored. Real connectivity meant running down the street to your friends' houses. You didn't need to be connected because it just wasn't possible then.

Your expectation for stimulation was also quite low. The most technological stimulation you had at your disposal was from television and radio. With so little artificial stimulation available, you were forced to stimulate yourselves with reading, games, sports, playing with your friends, and just plain using your own imagination.

Oh, how times have changed. Our digital natives have grown up in a world that has turned those expectations upside down and inside out. Today, connectivity is constant and instantaneous and so is the expectation for it to be that way. It's that expectation that has turned children from *wanting* to be connected back in the day to *needing* to be connected now. Also, the more connected children are, the more connectivity becomes a habit and habits are, in essence, needs that must be fulfilled.

Recent research has also shown that the need for connectivity isn't just psychological but rather has its basis in brain chemistry. As I discussed in chapter 9, the use of technology can trigger the same neurochemicals associated with drug use and gambling. Quite literally, children can become hooked on technology, which turns the desire for connectivity into a physiological need.

In addition, children of this generation no longer need to stimulate themselves. Instead, they have a veritable cornucopia of popular culture and technology to gain stimulation from, from old-school television and radio to video games, texting, Internet surfing, and social networking. As with connectivity, they have become accustomed to and, dare I say, hooked on experiencing stimulation through technology.

Kids 3.0 have a balanced relationship with technology that enables them to maintain control over its use. Early on, their parents established reasonable restrictions, provided supervision, and taught them other ways of feeling connected. As a consequence, Kids 3.0 don't experience the need to be connected through technology because they have learned to keep it in perspective and to maintain healthy expectations. Also, because of their limited and controlled exposure early in their lives, Kids 3.0 didn't develop the habits of overuse that create the need for connectivity. Instead, they see technology as a tool that is available when needed, not always needing to be used.

Kids 3.0 are primarily self-stimulators because their parents didn't allow them to become overstimulated by and dependent on technology for stimulation. Although they can enjoy the types of stimulation that both offer, such as television shows, online games, and texting, Kids 3.0 rely most often on old-school means of stimulation, such as reading, playing games, and participating in sports. They have not developed the attitudes, habits, or neurochemistry that will drive them to an overdependence on technology for stimulation.

The result is children who can enjoy popular culture and use technology to their fullest benefit for both connectivity and stimulation while not losing sight of the difference between want and need. Kids 3.0 keep their engagement with popular culture and technology in their proper perspective and, in doing so, are in control of the relationship rather than being controlled by the relationship.

Twenty-First-Century Thinkers

Ironically, unrestrained and unguided immersion into popular culture and technology actually hurts your children's chances to thrive in this crazy new world. As I have demonstrated throughout *Raising Generation Tech*, popular culture and technology have a huge impact on how children think, from the values and attitudes that guide their thinking to their perceptions, thoughts, and decisions that express their thinking.

Popular culture limits children's ability to think because it tells them what to think and how to think, all of which funnels directly to popular culture's interests, and not the interests of your children. Immersion in the shallowness and narrowness of, for example, celebrity, wealth, physical appearance, and entertainment, encourages a herd mentality, conformity, and mediocrity. Children who buy into popular culture tend to think dichotomously; life is either–or, black or white; people are either rich or poor, beautiful or ugly, powerful or weak. Popular culture loves this simplistic thinking because it can control the few choices that children are presented with and can restrict the number of decisions that children have to make. Popular culture shapes children to become narrow minded, uncreative, and poor decision makers because they view their world in a restricted way and neglect to see the depth and breadth that life has to offer.

Technology also encourages restricted thinking in children, though not with the ill intentions of popular culture. Rather, through its very nature and design, technology forces children into a box, albeit a very entertaining box, that offers only a certain number of options through its many buttons, pop-ups, and menus. These limited options result in inside-the-box thinking that prevents these children from engaging in the kind of thinking—open minded, creative, original—that are an absolute necessity for them to prosper in the twenty-first century.

By setting limits, offering guidance, and ensuring that popular culture and technology play only a small role in their lives, parents of Kids 3.0 ensure that their children are neither brainwashed by popular culture nor limited by tech think. Because popular culture and technology haven't placed them in a box, Kids 3.0 are capable of thinking that is receptive, unrestrained, expansive, and innovative. Kids 3.0 are able to see a wide spectrum of options available to them and can recognize, choose from, and experience the extremes of life and all points along its continuum. Kids 3.0 are also able to deal with the ambiguity and complexities of life that are always present because they're able to find novel and personal solutions to the challenges that they will inevitably face.

Caring

The growing epidemic of narcissism that I discussed in chapter 5 is driven by a popular culture that reveres selfishness, self-adoration, self-satisfaction, and indifference for others. Whether the self-promotion of reality TV stars, the self-absorption of professional athletes, or the self-important streams of meaningless tweets from celebrities, popular culture sends messages to children that they should only care about themselves. At a deeper level, this narcissism results in a loss of real connection with and empathy for others. In other words, children who come under the spell of narcissism just don't care about other people.

Technology also plays a role in the rise of narcissism among our young people. Despite the seeming connectedness of everyone these days, so much of technology, particularly social networking sites such as Facebook, is about self-presentation and attention getting rather than building healthy relationships.

This self-absorption, though clearly in vogue, is actually self-defeating because it leaves children unprepared for the crazy new world in which so many people are connected and *relationships*, *cooperation*, and *collaboration* are the buzzwords for success. Narcissistic children are focused on themselves and have a fundamental disregard for others. These children consistently act in ways that promote their own interests and either discount or undermine the interests of others. These children are spoiled, insensitive, needy, and generally irascible because they care only about themselves. As a result, they have difficulty establishing healthy relationships in all parts of their lives.

In contrast, Kids 3.0 haven't bought into the "it's all about me" hype from popular culture. Their parents made a concerted effort to protect them from these messages by limiting their exposure to popular culture. They also communicated decidedly different messages to their children that were aimed to counteract those of narcissism from popular culture and replace them with messages of unselfishness and caring.

Kids 3.0 also learn to use technology not as a means to market themselves but rather as a tool for building and maintaining substantial relationships based on shared values and interests. They use technology as a tool for real relationships with people they have just met, and they strengthen the connections that they already have with people who have been in their lives for some time.

Because their parents exposed them to many sharing and giving experiences, Kids 3.0 understand that real meaning, satisfaction, and joy don't come from the vacuous offerings of popular culture or the immediate gratification of technology. Rather, they know that fulfillment comes from caring, being deeply connected with others, and giving of themselves for the sake of others. The selflessness and caring that Kids 3.0 hold so dear enable them to meet their own appropriate needs while at the same time making those of other people a priority. This caring is expressed in every part of their lives, with family and friends, in school, and in the many activities they participate in. These children are caring, helpful, and supportive, because giving to others is one of their greatest joys. Kids 3.0 are the best defense against popular culture and technology because they offer an ethos of "it's all about others."

Self-Affirming

As I described in chapter 5, children who are unduly influenced by popular culture have been found to be vulnerable to low self-esteem. So much of their lives is built on receiving validation from others, whether through popular culture, peers, or the immediate affirmation that technology offers through tweets, text messages, and Facebook postings. When children constantly feel validated by popular culture and technology, they develop an overreliance on outside influences for their self-esteem. This dependence makes these children vulnerable to anyone or anything that will provide the much-needed validation. Popular culture is only too happy to help these children to feel good about themselves, if they will only buy the right gadgets, wear the right clothes, listen to the right music, and eat the right foods.

Gaining this external validation artificially and temporarily makes these children feel a bit better about themselves but does little to nourish their real self-esteem. It also leaves them less capable of affirming themselves through recognition of their own self-worth, relationships that they have, or their own accomplishments. These children are insecure, uncomfortable with themselves, and dependent because they don't feel good about themselves and because they rely on others to gain a sense of self-worth.

Kids 3.0 are raised in a family culture that doesn't allow that external validation from popular culture and technology to take hold. Instead, their parents showed them where their self-esteem should come from and how to gain affirmation for themselves. This upbringing has allowed Kids 3.0 to see themselves as loved, secure, and competent people who receive validation from appropriate others, such as family, friends, and teachers, but they also have the ability to affirm their own self-esteem. Kids 3.0 gain affirmation directly from the life experiences and relationships they engage in. This self-confirmation allows them to have greater control over their self-esteem and keeps them from having to seek out unhealthy sources of self-esteem, such as popular culture and technology, just to feel good about themselves. It also enables Kids 3.0 to be less vulnerable to popular culture's attempts at manipulating their self-esteem. Kids 3.0 are confident, contented, and independent because they are happy with who they are and can gain self-worth for themselves when needed.

Able to Have a Long-Term Perspective

Popular culture exerts its influence over children by keeping them focused on their most immediate wants and needs. With its constantly changing images and sounds, popular culture prevents children from seeing any further than the next brief, entertaining moment. Children who fall for this attraction are expressly concerned with the short term. This limited perspective causes them to rely on their most recent past experiences and the most immediate ensuing activities to determine what they think, how they feel, and the way in which they will behave.

Technology also plays a role in stifling this long-term perspective. One of the hallmarks of all forms of recent technology is immediacy and the ability to inhibit consideration of the future by constantly intervening with a steady flow of inputs (e.g., text messages, tweets) and outputs (e.g., responding to texts, tweets). The result is a feedback loop in which children become trapped in the now, lacking the time and focus to reflect on the past or consider the future.

These children often act in ways that are not in their best interests in the long run because their immediate interests, often not at all healthy, take precedence over their long-term well-being. These children are usually impatient, easily distracted, and make poor choices because they're always focused on the here and now and are unable to look into the future and take a long-term perspective.

The parents of Kids 3.0 make sure that their children don't fall victim to this myopia. They limit and guide their children's exposure to popular culture and technology that puts blinders on them. These parents also teach their children about patience, delayed gratification, and the importance of weighing immediate benefits with long-term ramifications.

This perspective, once instilled, enables Kids 3.0 to disregard the unhealthy messages and habits from popular culture and technology. It also helps them make better decisions because they're taking into account more relevant past, present, and future information. With this more expansive view of life, these children can recognize and accept the inevitable ups and downs of life. This attitude also allows them to stay focused on the joy of the journey of life without being overly concerned with immediate events that arise. These children are patient, deliberate, and better able to handle the normal stresses of life because the breadth of their view puts everything in that long-term perspective.

Able to Lead a Rich Life

Popular culture tries (and usually succeeds) these days to convince children that leading a rich life involves being wealthy, having a big house, driving expensive cars, wearing fancy clothes and jewelry, and traveling first class. That, I would argue, is a moneyed life, not a rich one.

In fact, extensive research on happiness agrees with me. Numerous studies have shown that, once our basic needs are met, additional money has little or no effect on our well-being. Other research has shown that people who hold a "materialistic value orientation" (MVO) actually report lower quality of life and happiness, poor relationships, more substance abuse problems, and they contribute less to their communities than those who don't hold such an orientation. Researchers also found that when the value of wealth, influence, and luxury takes precedence over other values, people indicate lower levels of well-being and increased behavioral problems. Strikingly, these findings begin to emerge in children; teenagers with an MVO have higher incidences of depression and anxiety, and college students with an MVO are more narcissistic, have lower self-esteem, have difficulty with relationships, and are more likely to abuse drugs.

If your children are immersed in popular culture without reasonable limits or appropriate supervision, they have little chance of resisting these messages. Popular culture's celebration of wealth and material excess will simply overwhelm your children if they are left on their own to confront these messages.

In addition, immersion in technology can preclude children from leading a rich life. Such a mediated life simply can't offer children the three-dimensional, multisensory, open-ended, value-driven, and truly connected experiences that I discussed in chapter 4 and that come from parents who truly understand what a rich life is and how to help their children develop it.

When I talk about a rich life, I'm suggesting a life not measured in monetary terms but rather one that is like a fine piece of cloth: intricately woven, textured, layered, interestingly patterned, and pleasing to the eye and to the touch. Parents of Kids 3.0 understand this and also recognize that such a life doesn't include being immersed unhealthily in popular culture and technology (though both can certainly be a part of a rich life).

Instead, a rich life is developed by offering children healthy values, attitudes, experiences, and relationships. A life as Kids 3.0 is just such a life and is expressed in the breadth, depth, and quality of children's psychological, social, and achievement lives. These days, however, because of the dominant influence of popular culture and technology in your children's lives, a rich life isn't a given but rather a gift. That gift can be given to you only if you deliberately and actively raise Kids 3.0. So, you may ask, what do I really mean by this gift of a rich life for which I advocate so strongly for your children?

A rich life expressed by Kids 3.0 is characterized by deep, satisfying, and lasting relationships with family, friends, schoolmates, coworkers, neighbors, and members of the community you live in. These connections are based on shared values, beliefs, interests, and activities. Healthy relationships offer love, caring, encouragement, emotional support, practical assistance, and stress release. These relationships give Kids 3.0 opportunities to reach out, connect, and give to others who, in turn, can give so much back to them. Relationships are high on the list of priorities for a rich life because of the robust finding that they are the single most important contributor to happiness.

A rich life is typified by activities Kids 3.0 have a passion for and with which they have a deep connection. School, hobbies, sports, the arts, hobbies, and cultural and religious activities provide them with experiences and challenges that can't be gained from popular culture or technology and give their lives true meaning by offering them satisfaction, joy, fun, inspiration, and pride.

A rich life is deep, diverse, and balanced. Kids 3.0 lead lives that are deeply involved in one or two activities yet are engaged in many. This diversity provides them with many sources of meaning and validation, and it gives them many directions to choose from in their life's journey. This variety of activities creates Kids 3.0 who have balanced self-identities and lives; if one area isn't going well, gratification in other areas sustains them.

A rich life is both comfortable and stimulating. Kids 3.0 feel a sense of comfort because their lives emerge from their most deeply held values. Kids 3.0 also experience a sense of contentment, security, and "I'm in a good place" because they control their lives rather than the disingenuous popular culture and technology that can engulf them. This comfort enables Kids 3.0 to be calm and at ease when they aren't doing anything and encourages them to pursue stimulation when they want it. Their comfort also prevents them from feeling compelled to seek stimulation from popular culture and technology out of boredom, need for acceptance, or validation.

From this place of security and comfort, Kids 3.0 can focus their energy and pursue their intellectual, physical, social, artistic, or spiritual interests with vigor. The experience of those interests acts to reenergize them and, at the same time, ground them in the feeling of comfort. Kids 3.0 are connected, enrapt, and stimulated in the healthiest ways as they immerse themselves in these interests, in contrast to the artificial and short-lived stimulation that popular culture and technology offer.

A rich life allows Kids 3.0 to dream. Because their thinking isn't restricted by the box that popular culture wants to place them in or by the limited options offered by technology, Kids 3.0 have the opportunity to find, identify, and pursue the dreams that emerge from their passions and interests. Kids 3.0 have a sense of security and support from their families that provides them with a safe haven from which they can explore their world. They also feel a sense of freedom and independence that inspires them to seek their dreams.

A rich life is hereditary. When I say "hereditary," I don't mean it in the usual sense of parents passing certain traits on to their children through their genes. Instead, I mean that parents of Kids 3.0 lead rich lives that are based on healthy values and attitudes and pass those on to their children, who observe who their parents are and what they do. Children are then constitutionally driven to create rich lives of their own. Just as abused children often repeat abuse when they become parents, Kids 3.0 are also likely to pass on their rich life to their children, and as a result, it is replicated and sustained across generations.

Loving of Self and Others

Kids 3.0 love themselves. I don't mean in the narcissistic and self-absorbed way that I described in chapter 5. Those children don't actually love themselves but rather are driven by the need to gain love and validation from others because it is genuine love they are starved for. Children with this unhealthy love are also incapable of loving others, which means that they don't receive the healthy love from others that they crave.

The self-love that Kids 3.0 feel is nourished by receiving love from others, feelings of safety, and confidence in their capabilities. It gives Kids 3.0 faith in who they are, what they believe, and how they want to live their lives. This healthy self-love puts children in a position of security and strength from which they can explore, take risks, and strive toward their goals. This love comes from parents who make love an essential value in their families and express healthy love to their children, resulting in children who don't need to seek love—even in its most shallow and unsatisfying form—from popular culture and peers. By experiencing healthy love from their parents, Kids 3.0 learn to love themselves and express their love for others in a positive way. This self-love allows them to be vulnerable and to have the comfort to express love to others without fear of rejection or condemnation.

This self-love and the ability to express emotions in a healthy way helps Kids 3.0 to develop loving relationships with others. The openness that other people sense from Kids 3.0 encourages them to reciprocate love and other nurturing emotions they feel toward these children. These emotional expressions foster deep connections between Kids 3.0 and others that bring them meaning, satisfaction, and happiness in their lives.

Masters of Their Lives

As I discussed previously, we live in a culture of acquiescence and conformity in which children, unaware of the consequences, unintentionally relinquish control of their lives in return for acceptance and immediate gratification. Many parents inadvertently enable this kidnapping of their children when they fail to protect them from or prepare them for their immersion into this crazy new world of popular culture and technology.

Perhaps the saddest result of this submission is that these children become victims with little ability to exert influence over their own lives. Children who are raised as victims have little self-regard, have no sense of responsibility, are fearful, believe they are powerless to change what they don't like, and are dependent on others to direct their lives. These children also lack initiative and creativity, so when they get bored or frustrated, they look to popular culture and technology for stimulation and solutions. Most painfully, children who are victims are entirely at the mercy of others and are helpless to effect change in their own lives.

Kids 3.0, by contrast, are raised to be masters of their lives with a strong sense of ownership and control. Their parents consciously limit their exposure to popular culture and technology and, as a result, don't succumb to their hypnotic allure. Parents of Kids 3.0 establish clear expectations and consequences, hold their children accountable for their actions, and require them to take initiative in their lives. This environment fosters self-esteem, responsibility, and decision-making capabilities. Kids 3.0 learn that they have the power to effect change in themselves and others. The most important benefit of this ability is that, when something is not going well in their lives, Kids 3.0 have the ability to make changes. This power is essential because our world is constantly in flux, and there are so many areas over which children have little control. Kids 3.0's belief in their ability to control their lives reduces doubt and fear when unwelcome changes occur, gives them confidence that they can make beneficial changes, and spurs them to make the necessary changes. This power enables Kids 3.0, when they leave the protection of the family, to resist the ever-present attraction of popular culture and technology and keep them in their proper perspective.

This sense of mastery also helps Kids 3.0 be better citizens of the world. Knowing that they have power over their own lives, Kids 3.0 also learn that they can positively influence others. This belief is so important because it allows these children to act on the values that they hold most dear and make meaningful contributions to others. Kids 3.0 don't see the world as a place in which others should serve them but rather as a place in which they can serve others.

Up on Popular Culture

You needn't worry that your Kids 3.0 will become social outcasts because they aren't up on the latest music, websites, social media, or reality TV shows (unless they choose not to be). Although Kids 3.0 show a range of interest in popular culture, from fascination to complete disregard, whatever appeal it holds for them is grounded in a healthy attitude toward and balanced engagement in it. In other words, Kids 3.0 are able to embrace and enjoy the entertainment value that popular culture has to offer while eschewing its seemingly siren's-call-like attraction and noxious messages. Popular culture is a part of their full life, but it never exerts an undue influence or takes up too much of their time at the cost of other more important pursuits. So Kids 3.0 can periodically play violent video games with their friends, spend time interacting with social media, and know the latest on reality TV shows without this involvement harming them in any way.

Not surprisingly, though, it has also been my observation that Kids 3.0 generally have considerably less interest in popular culture than do children who have been immersed in it with few limits and little guidance. Because popular culture didn't play a significant role in the upbringings of Kids 3.0, it usually doesn't register prominently on their radar screens.

This lack of immersion and engagement in popular culture has an impact on their social lives. Because they have different values and priorities from other children, Kids 3.0 often have limited interest in others who are deeply involved in popular culture, and they tend to seek out other children with similar sensibilities and interests. Thus, though they may have the ability to hang around the digital water cooler and chat it up about popular culture with their peers, they usually have better things to do with their time.

Tech Savvy

You also needn't worry that Kids 3.0 will be unprepared for the rigors of the digital world. Kids 3.0, by the very nature of their name, aren't going to be sixteenth- or even twentieth-century children living in the second millennium without the knowledge or skills to survive in this crazy new world. To the contrary, they will be even better equipped to prosper in this connected age than other children who may have been immersed in technology from an early age. Kids 3.0 will be more intellectually, psychologically, emotionally, and socially prepared for their wired experiences because their parents protected them with reasonable limits when they weren't developmentally ready to be immersed in that world. Then, as Kids 3.0 developed, their parents provided them with appropriate involvement with technology while instilling healthy attitudes and habits about its use. The result is children who have both the wherewithal and the capabilities to develop a healthy relationship with technology and to use it in a deliberate way to their greatest benefit.

Able to Have a Healthy Perspective on an Unhealthy World

Finally, one of the most important benefits of raising Kids 3.0 is that they have a healthy perspective on a decidedly unhealthy world. A sad reality of life these days is that it's not very kid friendly. Although popular culture and technology certainly have their benefits, more often they send children messages that do far more harm than good. The perspective that Kids 3.0 hold acts as a protective shield against everything that popular culture and technology tries to throw at them. It also works as a filter for everything that Kids 3.0 see, hear, think, feel, experience, and learn when they're engaged with popular culture and technology. This outlook gives them the ability to view the seductive messages of popular culture critically rather than being naively enticed by its bright lights, loud music, attractive people, and charismatic characters. This healthy view enables Kids 3.0 to see popular culture for what it is: a dishonest, manipulative, and unhealthy force that cares nothing for them but that, nonetheless, can offer entertainment value from time to time. This perspective allows Kids 3.0 to make deliberate choices about the popular culture they expose themselves to and how they use technology in their lives.

By raising Kids 3.0, you're giving your children the opportunity to decide for themselves how they choose to spend their time and direct their energy rather than being passive and powerless recipients of whatever popular culture and technology offers them. This healthy perspective that Kids 3.0 embrace from the culture that you create for them not only influences their relationships with popular culture and technology but, not surprisingly, also permeates and shapes important aspects of their lives, including their educational and career pursuits as well as their relationships, hobbies, and cultural activities.

This outlook, grounded in the values that you expose them to from an early age, ultimately determines what kind of people Kids 3.0 become. These true twenty-first-century children largely repudiate the harmful aspects of popular culture and technology while embracing their many benefits. The end result is children who mature into thoughtful, responsible, caring, and contributing members of our society whose values propel them to make the world a better place than it is now. I don't think any parent could ask for anything more than that in their children.

Raising Kids 3.0: Meet Your Kids 3.0

- Mature

- Value driven

- Able to distinguish need from want

- Twenty-first-century thinkers

- Caring

- Self-affirming

- Able to have a long-term perspective

- Able to lead a rich life

- Loving of self and others

- Masters of their lives

- Up on popular culture

- Tech savvy

- Able to have a healthy perspective on an unhealthy world

Afterword

When you raise Kids 3.0, you can take great pride and satisfaction in knowing that you're raising children who will be truly exceptional people in a culture in which mediocrity and conformity are the standard. You can also be heartened that the Kids 3.0 who you are raising have the capacity to help shape future generations and offer an alternative to the life that is dominated by popular culture and technology.

You may not fully appreciate the wonderful lifelong gifts that you give your children when you raise them to be Kids 3.0, protecting and preparing them for this crazy new world. You may not even notice the gifts because they will be so embedded in your children and so consistent with the values you immersed them in. The gifts are not just about what you see in your children; they're also about what you don't see. You'll see these gifts in what your children are not: selfish, greedy, disrespectful, angry, or uncaring. You won't notice what your children don't think, what they don't feel, what they don't say, and what they don't do. Your children may not even be aware of these gifts as they're growing up because the gifts have been so woven into your family, who they are, and the way they lead their lives.

These gifts will exert a profound influence over your children, coloring every aspect of their lives, directing, guiding, and shaping their thoughts, emotions, actions, decisions, and relationships throughout their lives; they will use popular culture and technology for their upsides while rejecting their downsides. Of course, you'll be aware of these gifts in their relationship with popular culture and technology. As your children mature into young adults, these gifts will come into even sharper relief in all aspects of their lives. You'll be able to see these gifts in all the ways in which your children live their lives: the values they express, the perspectives they hold, the quality of the life they establish for themselves, the way they treat themselves and others, and the way they use their gifts to contribute to the world. Quite powerfully, you'll see stark differences when your children are around other children who aren't fortunate enough to have been raised as Kids 3.0.

What is your reward for raising Kids 3.0? Well, certainly to see your children develop into just plain good human beings. At a much more basic level, at some point in your children's lives, they will recognize these gifts and say, "Thank you for all you've done and all you've given me." At that point, your heart will skip a beat and you'll get a lump in your throat. You'll think back to when your children were young and you made the commitment to raising them to be Kids 3.0. You'll smile and say, "You are most welcome."

References

American Academy of Child and Adolescent Psychiatry (2011, March). Obesity in children and teens. *Facts for Families.* www.aacap.org/galleries/FactsForFamilies/79_obesity_in_children_and_teens.pdf

American Psychological Association. (2006, March 20). *Multitasking: Switching costs.* www.apa.org/research/action/multitask.aspx

American Psychological Association, Task Force on the Sexualization of Girls. (2010). *Report of the APA Task Force on the Sexualization of Girls.* www.apa.org/pi/women/programs/girls/report-full.pdf

Anders, M. (2008, July–August). As good as the real thing? *ACE Fitness Matters.* www.acefitness.org/getfit/studies/WiiStudy.pdf

Appel, M. (2011, April–June). A story about a stupid person can make you act stupid (or smart): Behavioral assimilation (and contrast) as narrative impact. *Media Psychology, 14*(2), 144–167.

Ayduk, O., Gyurak, A., & Luerssen, A. (2009). Rejection sensitivity moderates the impact of rejection on self-concept clarity. *Personality and Social Psychology Bulletin, 35*(11), 1467-1478.

Baumrind, D. (1991). The influence of parenting style on adolescent competence and substance use. *Journal of Early Adolescence, 11*(1), 56–95.

Being a celebrity is the "best thing in the world" say children. (2006, December 18). *Mail Online News*. www.dailymail.co.uk/news/article-423273/Being-celebrity-best-thing-world-say-children.html

Benefits of sleep. (2011, November 20). www.better-sleep-better-life.com/benefits-of-sleep.html

Bennett, S., & Kalish, N. (2006). *The case against homework: How homework is hurting our children and what we can do about it.* New York: Crown.

Bishop, S. R., Lau, M., Shapiro, S., Carlson, L., Anderson, N. D., Carmody, J., et al. (2004). Mindfulness: A proposed operational definition. *Clinical Psychology: Science and Practice, 11*(3), 230–241.

Boneva, B. S., Quinn, A., Kraut, R. E., Kiesler, S., & Shklovski, I. (2006). Teenage communication in the instant messaging era. In R. Kraut, M. Brynin, & S. Kiesler (Eds.), *Information technology at home* (pp. 612–672). Oxford: Oxford University Press.

Bowker, A. (2009). Relationship between sports participation and self-esteem during early adolescence. *Canadian Journal of Behavioural Science. 38*(3), 214–229.

Boyd, D. M. (2007). Why youth (heart) social network sites: The role of networked publics in teenage social life (MacArthur Foundation Series on Digital Learning—*Youth, Identity, and Digital Media* volume). Cambridge, MA: MIT Press.

Boyd, D. M. (2008). *Taken out of context: American teen sociality in networked publics* (Unpublished doctoral dissertation, University of California, Berkeley). www.danah.org/papers/TakenOutOfContext.pdf

Brown, K. W., Kasser, T., Ryan, R. M., Linley, P. A., & Orzech, K. (2009). When what one has is enough: Mindfulness, financial desire discrepancy, and subjective well being. *Journal of Research in Personality*, *43*(5), 727–736.

Buckingham, D. (2007a). Childhood in the age of global media. *Children's Geographies*, *5*, 43–54.

Buckingham, D. (2007b). Selling childhood. *Journal of Children and Media*, *1*, 15–24.

Buijzen, M., & Valkenburg, P. M. (2003a). The effects of television advertising on materialism, parent-child conflict, and unhappiness: A review of research. *Applied Developmental Psychology*, *24*, 437–456.

Buijzen, M., & Valkenburg, P. M. (2003b). The unintended effects of television advertising: A parent-child survey. *Communication Research*, *30*(5), 483–503.

Burns, K. S. (2009). *Celeb 2.0: How social media foster our fascination with popular culture*. Santa Barbara, CA: Praeger/ABC-CLIO.

Burroughs, J. E., & Rindfleisch, A. (2002). Materialism and well-being: A conflicting values perspective. *Journal of Consumer Research*, *29*(3), 348–370.

Bushman, B. J. (1998). Priming effects of media violence on the accessibility of aggressive constructs in memory. *Personality and Social Psychology Bulletin*, *24*, 537–546.

Byun, S., Ruffini, C., Mills, J. E., Douglas, A. C., Niang, M., Stepchenkova, S., et al. (2009). Internet addiction: Metasynthesis of 1996–2006 quantitative research. *Cyberpsychology and Behavior*, *12*(2), 203–207.

Calvert, S. L. (2008). Children as consumers: Advertising and marketing. *Children and Electronic Media, 18*(1), 205–234.

Campbell, A. J., Cumming, S. R., & Hughes, I. (2006). Internet use by the socially fearful: addiction or therapy? *Cyberpsychology and Behavior, 9*(1), 69–81.

Carr, N. (2010, May 24). The Web shatters focus, rewires brains. *Wired*. www.wired.com/magazine/2010/05/ff_nicholas_carr/all/1

Chaplin, L. N., & John, D. R. (2005). Materialism in children and ado-lescents: The role of the developing self-concept. *Advances in Consumer Research, 32*, 219–220.

Cheng, J. (2010, March 4). About half of parents "friend" their kids on Facebook. *CNN*. www.cnn.com/2010/TECH/05/04/parents.facebook/index.html?hpt=Sbin

Clark, P. W., Martin, C. A., & Bush, A. J. (2001). The effect of role model influence on adolescents' materialism and marketplace knowl-edge. *Journal of Marketing Theory and Practice, 9*(4), 27–36.

Clay, D., Vignoles, V. L., & Dittmar, H. (2005). Body image and self-esteem among adolescent girls: Testing the influence of sociocultural factors. *Journal of Research on Adolescence, 15*(4), 451–477.

Clay, R. A. (2009, February). Mini-multitaskers. *APA Monitor, 4*(2), 38.

Common Sense Media. (2009). *Is social networking changing child-hood? A national poll.* San Francisco, CA: Common Sense Media. www.commonsensemedia.org/about-us/news/press-releases/social-networking-changing-childhood

Conger, K. (2006, April 12). Watch not, want not? Kid's TV time tied to consumerism. *Stanford University News*. news.stanford.edu/news/2006/april12/med-tv-041206.html

Considine, A. (2010, September 3). Defriended, not de-emoted. *New York Times*. www.nytimes.com/2010/09/05/fashion/05noticed.html

Cynopsis Media. (2011, August 19). *Cynopsis: Kids!* www.cynopsis.com/editions/kids/081911/

Davidson, R. J., Kabat-Zinn, J., Schumacher, J., Rosenkranz, M., Muller, D., Santorelli, S. F., et al. (2003). Alterations in brain and immune function produced by mindfulness meditation. *Psychosomatic Medicine*, *65*(3), 564–570.

Davila, J., Hershenberg, R., Feinstein, B., Starr, L. R., & Gorman, K. (2010, November). *Is use of social networking tools associated with depressive symptoms among youth?* Paper presented at the forty-fourth annual meeting of the Association for Behavioral and Cognitive Therapies, San Francisco, CA.

Davila, J., Stroud, C. B., Starr, L. R., Ramsay Miller, M., Yoneda, A., & Hershenberg, R. (2009). Romantic and sexual activities, parent-adolescent stress, and depressive symptoms among early adolescent girls. *Journal of Adolescence*, *32*, 909–924.

Educational Testing Center: Research Center. (1999). *Academic cheating fact sheet*. www.glass-castle.com/clients/www-nocheating-org/adcouncil/research/cheatingfactsheet.html

Eisenberger, N. I., Lieberman, M. D., & Williams, K. D. (2003). Does rejection hurt? An fMRI study of social exclusion. *Science*, *302*, 290–292.

eMarketer. (2010, November 9). *Is social media making consumers antisocial?* www.emarketer.com/Article.aspx?R=1008033

Experts debate Internet addiction. (2006, November 14). www.physorg.com/news82749930.html

"Facebook depression" seen as new risk for teens. (2011, March 28). *The Early Show.* www.cbsnews.com/stories/2011/03/28/earlyshow/living/parenting/main20047775.shtml

Family Safe Media. (2006). *Pornography statistics.* www.familysafemedia.com/pornography_statistics.html

Fang Gu, F., Hung, K., & Tse, D. K. (2005). Determinants for consumption materialism among late adolescents in china. In G. Menon & A. R. Rao (Eds.), *Advances in Consumer Research* (Vol. 32, pp. 649–650). Duluth, MN: Association for Consumer Research.

Finley, A. (2011). *Media and self esteem in girls.* kids.lovetoknow.com/wiki/Media_and_Self_Esteem_in_Girls

Flouri, E. (1999). An integrated model of consumer materialism: Can economic socialization and maternal values predict materialistic attitudes in adolescents? *Journal of Socioeconomics, 28,* 707–724.

Franzen, J. (2011, May 28). Liking is for cowards: Go for what hurts. *New York Times.* www.nytimes.com/2011/05/29/opinion/29franzen.html?pagewanted=2&_r=3&sq=liking%20is%20for%20cowards&st=cse&scp=1

Fredrickson, B. L., Cohn, M. A., Coffey, K. A., Pek, J., & Finkel, S. M. (2008). Open hearts build lives: Positive emotions, induced through loving-kindness meditation, build consequential personal resources. *Journal of Personality and Social Psychology, 95*(5), 1045–1062.

Friedman, W. (2011, September 23). *Toy Story*: Kid's ad market plays strong. *MediaPost News.* www.mediapost.com/publications/?fa=Articles. showArticle&art_aid=136312

Gantz, W., Schwartz, N., Angelini, J. R., & Rideout, V. (2007, March). *Food for thought: Television food advertising to children in the United States.* www.kff.org/entmedia/upload/7618.pdf

Gardner, A. (2007, December 5). Overweight kids often become obese, unhealthy adults. *US News.* health.usnews.com/usnews/health/ healthday/071205/overweight-kids-often-become-obese-unhealthy- adults.htm

Goldberg, M. E., & Gorn, G. (1978). Some unintended consequences of TV advertising to children. *Journal of Consumer Research, 5,* 22–29.

Goldberg, M. E., Gorn, G. J., Peracchio, L. A., & Bamossy, G. (2003). Understanding materialism among youth. *Journal of Consumer Psychology, 13*(3), 278–288.

Goleman, D., Boyatzis, R., & McKee, A. (2002). *Primal leadership: Realizing the power of emotional intelligence.* Boston: Harvard Business School Press.

Gonzales, A. L., & Hancock, J. T. (2011). Mirror, mirror on my Facebook wall: Effects of exposure to Facebook on self-esteem. *Cyberpsychology, Behavior, and Social Networking, 14*(1–2), 79–83.

Green, C. S., & Bavelier, D. (2003). Action video game modifies visual selective attention. *Nature, 423,* 534–537.

Green, C. S., & Bavelier, D. (2007). Action video game experience alters the spatial resolution of attention. *Psychological Science*, *18*(1), 88–94.

Greenfield, P. (2009). Technology and informal education: What is taught, what is learned. *Science*, *323*(5910), 69–71.

Greitemeyer, T., & Osswald, S. (2010). Effects of prosocial video games on prosocial behavior. *Journal of Personality and Social Psychology*, *98*(2), 211–221.

Harding, A. (2008, November 3). Violent video games linked to child aggression. *CNN*. articles.cnn.com/2008-11-03/health/healthmag.violent.video.kids_1_violent-video-video-games-game-genres/2?_s=PM:HEALTH

Hare, B. (2009, October 30). Defriending can bruise your "digital ego." *CNN*. edition.cnn.com/2009/TECH/science/10/30/online.rejection.defriending/index.html

Harris, J. R. (1995). Where is the child's environment? A group socialization theory of development. *Psychological Review*, *102*, 458–489.

Havrilesky, H. (2011, July 6). The divorce delusion. *New York Times*. www.nytimes.com/2011/07/10/magazine/the-divorce-delusion.html?pagewanted=3&_r=2&sq=kabuki%20%20mask&st=cse&scp=1

Hinchcliffe, D. (2006, November 5). *Web 2.0 definition updated and Enterprise 2.0 emerges*. www.zdnet.com/blog/hinchcliffe/web-20-definition-updated-and-enterprise-20-emerges/71

Italie, L. (2010, January 27). Tech use up with kids; parents losing ground. *MSNBC*. www.msnbc.msn.com/id/35099639/ns/technology_and_science-tech_and_gadgets/

Ito, M., Horst, H., Bittanti, M., Boyd, D., Herr-Stephenson, B., Lange, P. G., et al. (2008). *Living and learning with new media: Summary of findings from the Digital Youth Project* (John D. and Catherine T. MacArthur Foundation Reports on Digital Media and Learning). Chicago: John D. and Catherine T. MacArthur Foundation. digitalyouth.ischool.berkeley.edu/files/report/digitalyouth-TwoPageSummary.pdf

Jayson, S. (2007, January 10). Generation Y's goal? Wealth and fame. *USA Today*. www.usatoday.com/news/nation/2007-01-09-gen-y-cover_x.htm

Joseph Institute Center for Youth Ethics. (2011, February 10). *Installment 2: Honesty and integrity: What would honest Abe Lincoln say?* charactercounts.org/programs/reportcard/2010/installment02_report-card_honesty-integrity.html

Kasser, T. (2002). *The high price of materialism.* Cambridge, MA: MIT Press.

Kasser, T., & Ryan, R. (1993). A dark side of the American dream: Correlates of financial success as a central life aspiration. *Journal of Personality and Social Psychology, 65,* 410–422.

Kasser, T., & Ryan, R. M. (1996). Further examining the American dream: Differential correlates of intrinsic and extrinsic goals. *Personality and Social Psychology Bulletin, 22,* 280–287.

Kasser, T., & Ryan, R. (2001). Be careful what you wish for: Optimal functioning and the relative attainment of intrinsic and extrinsic goals. In P. Schmuck, & K. M. Sheldon (Eds.), *Life Goals and Well-Being: Towards a Positive Psychology of Human Striving* (pp. 116-133). Cambridge, MA: Hogrefe & Huber.

Kasser, T., Ryan, R. M., Couchman, C. E., & Sheldon, K. M. (2004). Materialistic values: Their causes and consequences. In T. Kasser & A. D. Kanner (Eds.), *Psychology and consumer culture: The struggle for a good life in a materialistic world* (pp. 11–28). Washington, DC: American Psychological Association.

Kasser, T., Ryan, R. M., Zax, M., & Sameroff, A. J. (1995). The relations of maternal and social environments to late adolescents' materialistic and prosocial values. *Developmental Psychology, 31*, 907–914.

Keim, B. (2009, August 24). Multitasking muddles brains, even when the computer is off. *Wired*. www.wired.com/wiredscience/2009/08/multitasking/

Kohn, A. (2006). *The homework myth: Why our kids get too much of a bad thing*. Cambridge, MA: Da Capo Press.

Kranzberg, M. (1986). Technology and history: "Kranzberg's Laws." *Technology and Culture, 27*(3), 544–560.

LaRose, R., Lin, C. A., & Eastin, M. S. (2003). Unregulated Internet usage: Addiction, habit, or deficient self-regulation? *Media Psychology, 5*(3), 225–253.

Lin, J. (2008, October 15). Research shows that Internet is rewiring our brains. *UCLA Today*. www.today.ucla.edu/portal/ut/081015_gary-small-ibrain.aspx

Lohaus, A., Ball, J., Klein-Hessling, J., & Wild, M. (2005). Relations between media use and self-reported symptomatology in young adolescents. *Anxiety, Stress, and Coping: An International Journal, 18*(4), 333–341.

Martin, C., & Bush, A. (2000). Do role models influence teenager's purchase intentions and behavior? *Journal of Consumer Marketing, 17*, 441–451.

Martin, D. (2009, November 22). Child's play. *Los Angeles Times.* articles.latimes.com/2009/nov/22/entertainment/la-ca-kids -celebrity22-2009nov22

McClements, M. (2010, December 31). "I took my kids offline." *Guardian.* www.guardian.co.uk/lifeandstyle/2011/jan/01/technology-ban-kids -home-experiment

McGivern, R. F., Andersen, J., Byrd, D., Mutter, K. L., & Reilly, J. (2002). Cognitive efficiency on a match to sample task decreases at the onset of puberty in children. *Brain and Cognition, 50*(1), 73–89.

McLuhan, M. (1964). *Understanding media: The extensions of man.* New York: McGraw Hill.

Mehdizadeh, S. (2010). Self-presentation 2.0: Narcissism and self-esteem on Facebook. *Cyberpsychology, Behavior, and Social Networking, 13*(4), 357–364.

Miller, E. K., Freedman, D. J., & Wallis, J. D. (2002). The prefrontal cortex: Categories, concepts and cognition. *Philosophical Transactions of the Royal Society B: Biological Sciences, 357*(1424), 1123–1136.

Moreno, R., & Mayer, R. (1999). Cognitive principles of multimedia learning: The role of modality and contiguity. *Journal of Educational Psychology, 91*(2), 358–368.

Multitasking may not mean higher productivity. (2009, August 28). *NPR.* www.npr.org/templates/story/story.php?storyId=112334449&ft =1&f=5

Narcissistic personality disorder. (2006). www.healthyplace.com/other-info/ psychiatric-disorder-definitions/narcissistic-personality-disorder/

National Center on Addiction and Substance Abuse at Columbia University. (2011, August 24). *National Survey of American Attitudes on Substance Abuse XVI: Teens and Parents.* www.casacolumbia.org/ templates/PressReleases.aspx?articleid=650&zoneid=87

National Sleep Foundation. *Bedroom poll: Summary of findings.* www .sleepfoundation.org/sites/default/files/bedroompoll/NSF_Bedroom _Poll_Report.pdf

Nault, K. (2005, November 2). *Teenage girls + media = low self-esteem.* ezinearticles.com/?Teenage-Girls-+-Media-=-Low-Self-Esteem&id =96389

Neuman, W. (2011, April 28). U.S. seeks new limits on food ads for children. *New York Times.* www.nytimes.com/2011/04/29/ business/29label.html?_r=1&scp=4&sq=junk%20food%20 children%20ads%20web%20sites&st=cse

Novotney, A. (2010, November). Surviving the media onslaught. *APA Monitor, 41*(10), 32.

Novotney, A. (2011, June). Beat the cheat. *Monitor on Psychology, 42*(6), 54–57.

O'Keeffe, G. S., & Clarke-Pearson, K. (2011). The impact of social media on children, adolescents, and families. *Pediatrics, 127*(4), 800–804.

Olds, T. S., Maher, C. A., & Matricciani, L. (2011). Sleep duration or bedtime? Exploring the relationship between sleep habits and weight status and activity patterns. *Sleep, 14*, 135–146.

Ophir, E., Nass, C., & Wagner, A. D. (2009). Cognitive control in media multitaskers. *Proceedings of the National Academy of Sciences of the United States of America*, *106*(37), 15583–15587.

O'Roarty, A. (2011, May 14). My kids don't watch TV (but I'm not judging you!). *Huffington Post*. www.huffingtonpost.com/abi-cotler-oroarty/kids-tv_b_848864.html

Pacific Council on International Policy. (2007). Disney President and CEO Robert A. Iger Says Brand Depth, Not Breadth, is Key to Effective Globalization. www.prnewswire.com/news-releases/disney-president-and-ceo-robert-a-iger-says-brand-depth-not-breadth-is-key-to-effective-globalization-57973182.html

Padilla-Walker, L. M. (2006). "Peers I can monitor, it's media that really worries me!" Parental cognitions as predictors of proactive parental strategy choice. *Journal of Adolescent Research*, *21*(1), 56–82.

Padilla-Walker, L. M., Nelson, L. J., Carroll, J. S., & Jensen, A. C. (2010). More than just a game: Video game and Internet use during emerging adulthood. *Journal of Youth and Adolescence*, *39*, 103–113.

Paul, P. (2012, January 22). Cracking teenagers' online codes. *New York Times*. www.nytimes.com/2012/01/22/fashion/danah-boyd-cracking-teenagers-online-codes.html?_r=1&scp=1&sq=danah%20boyd&st=cse

Pew Research Center. (2007, January). *How young people view their lives, futures, and politics: A portrait of "generation next."* www.people-press.org/files/legacy-pdf/300.pdf

Pigeron, E. (2010). "Positive effects of media on family interactions." Paper presented at the International Communication Association Annual Conference, Singapore.

Pytel, B. (2007, September 16). *Cheating is on the rise: Surveys show less integrity among high school and college students.* www.suite101.com/content/cheating-is-on-the-rise-a31238

Quenqua, D. (2010, April 28). Graduating from Lip Smackers. *New York Times.* www.nytimes.com/2010/04/29/fashion/29tween.html

Rettinger, D. A., & Kramer, Y. (2009). Situational and personal causes of student cheating. *Research in Higher Education, 50*(3), 293–313.

Richtel, M. (2010, November 21). Growing up digital, wired for distraction. *New York Times.* www.nytimes.com/2010/11/21/technology/21brain.html?_r=1&scp=1&sq=growing%20up%20digital&st=cse

Richtel, M. (2011, April 20). In online games, a path to young consumers. *New York Times.* www.nytimes.com/2011/04/21/business/21marketing.html?_r=3&hp

Rosen, C. (2007). Virtual friendship and the new narcissism. *New Atlantis, 17*, 15–31.

Rosen, L. D. (2011, August). *Poke me: How social networks can both help and harm your kids.* Invited presentation, annual convention of the American Psychological Association, Washington, DC.

Rosen, L. D., Cheever, N. A., & Carrier, L. M. (2008). The association of parenting style and child age with parental limit setting and adolescent MySpace behavior. *Journal of Applied Developmental Psychology, 29*(6), 459–471.

Roskos-Ewoldsen, D. R., Roskos-Ewoldsen, B., & Dillman Carpentier, F. R. (2002). Media priming: A synthesis. In J. Bryant & D. Zillmann (Eds.), *Media effects: Advances in theory and research* (pp. 97–115). Mahwah, NJ: Erlbaum.

Schwartzberg, J. (2011, August 22). Girls and *Jersey Shore*: An unparalleled mismatch. *Huffington Post*. www.huffingtonpost.com/joel-schwartzberg/jersey-shore-ratings_b_931629.html

Shackford, S. (2001, March 1). Our Facebook walls boost self-esteem, study finds. *Chronicle Online*. www.news.cornell.edu/stories/March11/FacebookMirrorStudy.html

Shao, R. P., & Skarlicki, D. P. (2009). The role of mindfulness in predicting individual performance. *Canadian Journal of Behavioral Science*, *41*(4), 195–201.

Shavelson, R. J., & Bolus, R. (1982). Self-concept: The interplay of theory and methods. *Journal of Educational Psychology*, *74*, 3–17.

Shavelson, R. J., Hubner, J. J., & Stanton, G. C. (1976). Self-concept: Validation of construct interpretations. *Review of Educational Research*, *46*, 407–441.

Small, G., Vorgan, G. (2011, February 18). Is the Internet killing empathy? *CNN*. www.cnn.com/2011/OPINION/02/18/small.vorgan.internet.empathy/index.html?hpt=C2

Song, I., Larose, R., Eastin, M. S., & Lin, C. A. (2004). Internet gratifications and Internet addiction: On the uses and abuses of new media. *CyberPsychology and Behavior*, *7*(4), 384–394.

Sparrow, B., Liu, J., & Wegner, D. M. (2011, July 14). Google effects on memory: Cognitive consequences of having information at our fingertips. *Science*. www.sciencemag.org/content/early/2011/07/13/science.1207745

Stefanone, M. A., Lackaff, D., & Rosen, D. (2011). Contingencies of self-worth and social-networking-site behavior. *Cyberpsychology, Behavior, and Social Networking, 14*(1–2), 41–49.

Stevens, S. B., & Morris, T. L. (2007). College dating and social anxiety: Using the Internet as a means of connecting to others. *CyberPsychology and Behavior, 10*(5), 680–688.

Stites, T. (2006, July 9). Modern love: Someone to watch over me (on a Google Map). *New York Times.* www.nytimes.com/2006/07/09/fashion/sundaystyles/09love.html?ei=5087&en=8b620a9c24917a7d&ex=1152590400&pagewanted=print

Strickland, J. (2006, July 7). *Is there a Web 1.0?* www.computer.howstuffworks.com/web-101.htm

Sweller, J. (1988). Cognitive load during problem solving: Effects on learning. *Cognitive Science, 12*(2), 257–285.

Taylor, J. (2009). *Psychology of technology: The evolution of connectivity.* www.drjimtaylor.com/blog/2009/08/psychology-of-technology-the-evolution-of-connectivity/

Uhls, Y. T., & Greenfield, P. M. (2011). The rise of fame: An historical content analysis. *Cyberpsychology: Journal of Psychosocial Research on Cyberspace, 5*(1), article 1.

University of Florida (1998, November 18). UF researcher: Participating in sports gives girls strong self-images. *ScienceDaily*. www.sciencedaily.com/releases/1998/11/981117150259.htm

University of Minnesota. (2008, June 21). Educational benefits of social networking sites uncovered. *Science Daily*. www.sciencedaily.com/releases/2008/06/080620133907.htm

University of Missouri-Columbia. (2007, February 2). Less television, more gathering around dinner table prevents kids from becoming overweight. *ScienceDaily*. www.sciencedaily.com/releases/2007/01/070131112409.htm

Valkenburg, P. M., & Peter, J. (2011). Online communication among adolescents: An integrated model on its attraction, opportunities, and risks. *Journal of Adolescent Health*, *48*, 121–127.

Walsh, S. P., White, K. M., & Young, R. M. (2010). Needing to connect: The effect of self and others on young people's involvement with their mobile phones. *Australian Journal of Psychology*, *62*, 194–203.

Ward, L., Epstein, M., Caruthers, A., & Merriwether, A. (2011). Men's media use, sexual cognitions, and sexual risk behavior: Testing a mediational model. *Developmental Psychology*, *47*(2), 592–602.

Warzak, W. J., Evans, S., Floress, M. T., Gross, A. C., & Stoolman, S. (2011). Caffeine consumption in young children. *Journal of Pediatrics*, *158*(3), 508–509.

WebMD Health News. (2006, April 4). *Media messages harm child, teen health*. www.webmd.com/parenting/news/20060403/media-messages-harm-child-teen-health?page=3

Weinschenk, S. (2009, November 7). *100 things you should know about people: #8, Dopamine makes you addicted to seeking information.* www.what makesthemclick.net/2009/11/07/100-things-you-should-know-about-people-8-dopamine-makes-us-addicted-to-seeking-information/

Weinstein, A., & Lejoyeux, M. (2010). Internet addiction or excessive Internet use. *American Journal of Drug and Alcohol Abuse, 36*(5), 277–283.

Who discovered electricity? (2011, September 7). *Wisegeek.* www.wise geek.com/who-discovered-electricity.htm

Wikipedia. *The Hub (TV network).* en.wikipedia.org/wiki/The_Hub_(TV _network)

Williams, K. D., Cheung, C. K. T., & Choi, W. (2000). Cyberostracism: Effects of being ignored over the Internet. *Journal of Personality and Social Psychology, 79,* 748–762.

Williams, K. D., & Warburton, W. A. (2003). Ostracism: A form of indirect aggression that can result in aggression. *International Review of Social Psychology, 16,* 101–126.

Williams, S. *Self-awareness and personal development.* www.wright.edu/~ scott.williams/LeaderLetter/selfawareness.htm

Wong, Y. C. (2010). Cyber-parenting: Internet benefits, risks and parenting issues. *Journal of Technology in Human Services, 28*(4), 252–273.

Xiuqin, H., Huimin, Z., Mengchen, L., Jinan, W., Ying, Z., & Ran, T. (2010). Mental health, personality, and parental rearing styles of adolescents with Internet addiction disorder. *Cyberpsychology, Behavior, and Social Networking, 13*(4), 401–406.

Zadro, L., Williams, K. D., & Richardson, R. (2004). How low can you go? Ostracism by a computer lowers belonging, control, self-esteem and meaningful existence. *Journal of Experimental Social Psychology, 40,* 560–567.

Acknowledgments

I can't adequately convey the debt of gratitude that I owe Stephanie Dargoltz for her contributions to *Raising Generation Tech*. Clearly, she is a glutton for punishment, as this book is her second as my research assistant. But seriously, the timely completion and quality of this book wouldn't have been possible without her commitment, professionalism, eye for detail, and follow-through. It was a pleasure and a privilege working with her on *Raising Generation Tech*.

I have thanked Stephanie countless times for all she has done for me, but I won't ever be able to thank her enough. But, just to ensure that she gets my message, I will thank her one more time. So, Stephanie, thank you, thank you, thank you from the bottom of my heart. I have just one question for you. Are you available for my next parenting book?!

Index

A

Activities for children
  involvement, 90
Advertising, 5
Advertising industry, 28–29
Attentional ability, 120
Authoritative parents, 210
Avarice culture, 98

B

Baby boomers, 161
Bad values, 112
Balanced childhood, 71
Boredom, 201
Boundaries for well-being, 16
Brain chemistry, 237
Building community, 114

C

Capitulating parents, 45
Caring
  actively create, 115
  kids 3.0, 239–241
Cheating, 98–99
Chicken Little, 2
  attitude, 18
  view of popular culture and
    technology, 20
Children
  attracted to distractions, 141
  boxed in by technology, 65–66
  consumers, 28–30
  controlling flow of information,
    124
  decide about values, 108–109
  decision-making process, 131
  defined, 9

exposed to bad value messages,
  56
external identity, 82
feel values, 107–108
healthy relationship with
  technology, 50
immerse in single activity, 128
independence from parents'
  involvement in social lives, 155
influence from popular culture
  and technology, 10
interact with values, 109–110
intrinsic passions and strengths,
  89
knowledge of popular culture, 31
overscheduled lives, 140
parents joining children in
  cyberspace, 156
physical well-being, 16
protect and prepare, 73–206
protecting from influence of
  popular culture, 213
real life offers open ended
  experiences, 66
relationships, 147
relationships with technology,
  46–47
seeing identities, 79
social world, 77

software, 11–13
supervising their media exposure,
  25
susceptible to unhealthy
  messages, 60
talk and listen to, 91
technology effect, 118
technology's influence, 2
think before acting, 136
vast changes, 1
Communications
advances, 34–35
common, 36
family, 154
technology, 34–36
Community
active, 115
building, 114
Complex relationship, 10–11
Crazy new world, 23–72
popular culture today, 25–32
setting defaults in your children,
  53–61
technology today, 33–51
unmediated life worth living,
  62–72
Critical thinking, 80
Culture of avarice, 98
Cyberbullying, 131

D

Decision making
best interests, 136
consequences of actions, 136
dreadful, 133
options, 136
popular culture, 133
skillful, 135
technological advances, 132
thinking, 130–134
Default concept, 53–61
attitudes, 56–57
development, 55
develop only positive, 59
free time and play, 57–58
physical, 57
power, 54
settings for children, 54, 55
social, 58
values, 55–56
Defriending, 159
Digital immigrants, 1, 155
Disconnecting
advantages, 226–228
parenting, 225–228
Distractions, 141, 142
children attracted to, 141
focus and minimize, 129
students, 127

Dolls, 30
Dorsey, Jack, 42

E

Emotional well-being boundaries,
16
Empathy, 152
Ends justify means attitude, 98

F

Facebook
depression, 175–176
formation and maintenance of
self-esteem in children, 83
Family
communications, 154
connectedness with popular
culture, 178
lifestyle, 90
relationships, 154–157
Family-value culture, 110
creation, 105–106
Faulty decision, 135
Focused on task, 141
Friendships
pursuit, 157
relationships, 157–159

G

Generation X, 161
Girls expectations, 30
Good values, 112
Greenfield, Susan, 192

H

Hard work and payoff, 207–254
  kids 3.0, 231–254
  parenting, 209–229
Health
  caution, 167–168
  eating, 180–181
  exercise, 182–183
  good influences from social
    media, 177–179
  high-risk behavior, 170–171
  junk food, 169–170
  kids 3.0, 179–180
  kids 3.0 and mental health,
    186–187
  kids 3.0 and physical health,
    180–186
  lack of exercise, 168–169
  mental health, 171–177
  physical, 168–170
  protect and prepare your
    children, 167–187
  skeptics, 224–225
  sleep, 183–186
Healthy activities for children
  involvement, 90
High-res life, 70–71
Homework, 184–185
Human
  development, 119
  interactions, 69
Hyperparenting, 86

I

IGeneration, 161
Influential contributors to
  children's development, 94
Information
Healthy activities for children
  involvement, 90
  available at children's fingertips,
    121
  help children control flow, 124
  overload, 121–123
  value, 122
Informed decisions, 19
Inoculate children against popular
  culture, 89
Intellectual well-being boundaries,
  16

Internet, 35
  addiction, 174–175
  formation and maintenance of
    self-esteem in children, 83
Invincibility, 100
IPhone syndrome, 198–202

J
Junk food, 169–170

K
Kids 3.0
  caring, 239–241
  decision making, 135–137
  defined, 13–14
  distinguishing need from want,
    235–238
  eating, 180–181
  engagement with popular
    culture, 250
  exercise, 182–183
  healthy perspective on unhealthy
    world, 251–252
  information, 124–125
  leading a rich life, 244–247
  and life, 202–205
  long-term perspective, 242–244
  loving self and others, 247–248

masters of their lives, 248–249
maturity, 233–234
mental health, 186–187
mindfulness, 142–144
payoff, 20–21
physical health, 180–186
raising by setting defaults, 61
raising through thinking, 144
raising through unmediated life,
    72
raising to know technology, 51
raising with popular culture, 32
raising with values, 115–116
reality, 89–90
relationship with popular culture,
    31–32
relationship with technology,
    48–51
self-affirming, 241–242
self-identity, 87–92
single tasking, 129–130
sleep, 183–186
tech savvy, 251
thinking, 134–138
twenty-first century thinkers,
    238–239
value driven, 234
values, 104–111

L

Life's meaning, 189–206
  iPhone syndrome, 198–202
  kids 3.0, 202–205
  virtual *vs.* real life, 190–194
  what children miss, 197–198
  wired but disconnected, 194–196
Limitations, 203–204
Listen to children, 91

M

Male-oriented media, 80
Materialism values, 100–102
Maturity, 233–234
McLuhan, Marshall, 7, 48
Media
  abstention, 173–174
  supervising children's exposure, 25
Mediated life and technology
  limitations, 191
Meeting kids 3.0, 238–252. *See also* Kids 3.0
  caring, 239–241
Mental health, 171–177, 186–187
  case study, 172–174
  Facebook depression, 175–176
  Internet addiction, 174–175
  Internet attraction, 176–177

Mindfulness, 138–142
  defined, 139
  steps to create, 143
Mobile phone technology, 35
Multitasking, 37, 39, 143
  defined, 126
  retain information, 126
  thinking, 125–129
  understanding, 128–129
Myopia, 243

N

Narcissism, 150, 239–240
  self-identity, 84–87
Narcissistic Personality Inventory, 85
Needs defined, 172
Net generation communication
  preference, 161
Nutrition, 180–181

O

Offline friendships, 157
Omnipresent popular culture and
  technology, 146
Online communications, 149
Online relationships
  attraction, 151–152
  benefits, 162

bubble of safety, 151
reality, 148–150
Opportunity costs, 41
Outdoor activities, 169
Overscheduled lives children, 140
Ownership, 249

P

Parenting
absentia, 44
active involvement, 212–213
children guidance as to use of
technology, 49
deconstruct popular culture and
technology, 215–216
disconnect, 39–41, 225–228
establish consequences, 220–223
establish limits, 217–219
expediency, 198–200
gatekeepers, 216–217
hard work and payoff, 209–229
joining children in cyberspace,
156
picking battles, 223–224
power, 8–10
raising health skeptics, 224–225
relationships with technology, 46
relationship with popular culture
and technology, 211–212

setting expectations for children,
219–220
study of popular culture and
technology, 213–215
Patience, 201
Person and persona line between,
79
Physical health, 168–170, 180–186
activities, 183
children, 16
eating, 180–181
exercise, 182–183
unmediated life worth living,
68–69
Pinsky, Drew, 85
Popular culture
avenues for communicating its
value messages, 96
children as consumers, 28–30
children's knowledge of popular
culture, 31
children's relationships, 147
crazy new world, 25–32
defined, 3, 26
degree of influence on children,
10
empathy, 179
engagement, 250

enhancing family connectedness, 178

inoculate children against, 89

kids 3.0 relationship with popular culture, 31–32

manipulation, 28

messages of wealth and materialism, 101

not all popular culture is bad, 27–28

omnipresent, 146

power, 3–7

setting expectations, 219–222

sexualization of girls, 30–31

shield children from corrosive values, 104

vs. synthetic culture, 5

unhealthy messages, 214

value messages, 103

values, 95–97

Private and public line between, 79

Programming value messages, 102

Protect and prepare your children, 73–206

health, 167–187

life's meaning, 189–206

relationships, 145–166

self-identity, 75–92

thinking, 117–144

values, 93–116

Psychological well-being

boundaries, 16

R

Raising kids 3.0. *See* Kids 3.0

Reading, 120

Reality

grounded, 89–90

Reality TV, 96

TV, 189–190

Real life

complications, 193

offers open ended experiences for children, 66

physical, 68

and values, 67

Relationships

caution, 162–166

competence, 196

complex, 10–11

defined, 145

defriending, 159

educate, 164

family, 154–157

family relationships, 154–157

friendships, 157–159

keys, 152–154

kids 3.0, 161–162

limits, 163–164

model healthy relationships, 164–165

online relationships attraction, 151–152

online relationships reality, 148–150

perception, 36

protect and prepare your children, 145–166

research, 159–161

rules and practices, 146

social experiences, 165–166

and technology, 150

unmediated life worth living, 69–70

Resolution, 70

S

Self-absorption, 239–240

Self-adoration, 86

Self-affirming, 241–242

Self-esteem, 236

  movement, 86

  self-identity, 83–84

Self-identity

  children, 79

create healthy family lifestyle, 90

emphasize healthy values, 88

exemplify healthy self-identity, 92

externalization, 76–80, 81

false self creation, 81–83

have children involved in healthy activities, 90

healthy, 76

help others, 91

highlight children's intrinsic passions and strengths, 89

inoculate children against popular culture's messages, 89

keep children grounded in reality, 89–90

kids 3.0, 87–92

primed children, 80–81

raising with self-identity, 92

rising narcissism, 84–87

self-esteem, 83–84

self-observation and information from social world, 76

surround children with healthy people, 90–91

talk and listen to children, 91

technology to expression, 78

Selflessness, 152

Self-love, 248

Sensory

experiences, 65

overload, 195

Setting defaults in your children,
53–61. *See also* Default concept

default development, 55

default power, 54

default types, 55–58

no guarantees, but, 59

parents defaults, 59–61

Sext messages, 131

Sexual activity and television, 171

Sexualization of girls, 30–31

Sexual predators online, 40

Shield children from corrosive
values, 104

Single activity for children, 128

Single tasking, 129–130

Social anxiety, 177

Social experiences, 165–166

Social media

good influences, 177–179

networking and offline
friendships, 157

sites and teenagers access, 38

use, 8

Social well-being boundaries, 16

Students distraction, 127

Supersystem, 28

Synthetic culture, 26

defined, 6

vs. popular culture, 5

T

Talk and listen to children, 91

Technology

attention to information, 119

cautionary tales, 43–46

change, 36–37

defined, 7

degree of influence on children,
10

effects on children, 118

empathy, 179

forcing children into box, 239

future, 47–48

harming relationships, 150

increase attentional ability, 120

influence on children, 2

kids 3.0 relationship with
technology, 48–51

law of unintended consequences,
41–43

limiting children, 65–66

lost opportunities, 41

omnipresent, 146

parent-child disconnect, 39–41

past, 33–35

power, 7–8

pursuit of friendship, 157

vs. thinking, 123

your family's relationship with
technology, 46–47

Tech savvy kids 3.0, 251

Teenagers access to social media
sites, 38

Television

programming value messages,
102

and sexual activity, 171

viewing results, 102

Text messages, 83

Thinking, 134–138

attention, 118–121

· coach good decision making,
137–138

decision making, 130–134

defined, 117

information overload, 121–123

kids 3.0 information, 124–125

kids 3.0 mindfulness, 142–144

kids 3.0 single tasking, 129–130

learning to make good decisions,
135–137

making bad decisions, 134–135

mindfulness, 138–142

multitasking, 125–129

protect and prepare your
children, 117–144

raise good decision makers, 138

vs. technology, 123

understanding multitasking,
128–129

Time

meaningful activities, 163–164

perception and relationships, 36

Twenty-first century thinkers,
238–239

U

Unmediated life, 64–70

choosing life for your children,
71

complete sensory experiences, 65

context, 67–68

high-res life, 70–71

open-ended experiences, 65–66

physicality, 68–69

relationships, 69–70

three dimensions of life, 64–65

values, 66–67

worth living, 64–70

Unprincipled attitude toward
success, 100

V

Value(s), 104–111, 111–115
  bad, 97–104
  connection with real life, 67
  consequences, 112
  create family-value culture,
    105–106
  dilemmas, 112–113
  exemplify values, 106
  fame, 102–104
  healthy, 95
  importance, 94–95
  influential contributors to your
    children's development, 94
  information, 122
  let children decide about values,
    108–109
  let children encounter values,
    110
  let children feel values, 107–108
  let children interact with values,
    109–110
  let children live values, 110–111
  neutral advancements, 148
  popular culture, 95–97
  protect and prepare your
    children, 93–116
  set limits, 111–112
  success at any cost, 97–100
  surround children with value-
    driven people, 113–115
  talk about values, 106–107
  unhealthy, 95
  wealth and materialism, 100–102
Value driven
  experiences, 110
  kids 3.0, 234
  people building community, 114
Video games
  children between ages of twelve
    and seventeen, 38
  growth, 29
Viewing television
  programming value messages,
    102
  results, 102
Virtual reality, 148
Virtual relationships, 148
Visual media, 120

W

Wealth and materialism values,
  100–102
Web 2.0, 12
Web 3.0, 12
Win at all costs mentality, 98

Working parent, 154
Workspace comfortable and
 organized, 130

Y
Young people's time, 37–38

Z
Zeitgeist of popular culture, 153

About the Author

Jim Taylor, PhD, has published more than 500 articles in scholarly and popular publications; has appeared on NBC's *Today Show*, ABC's *World News This Weekend*, and major television network affiliates; and has given more than 700 workshops and presentations throughout North America and Europe. He is the author of eight books, including *Positive Pushing: How to Raise a Successful and Happy Child*. An expert on the psychology of technology, Dr. Taylor blogs on numerous sites, including *Huffington Post*, *Psychology Today*, and *Fast Company*.